The Human Design Cult

The Human Design Cult

Jonah Dempcy

PLUNGE SANTA FE

THE HUMAN DESIGN CULT

First Plunge Edition: 2025

ISBN: 978-1-969429-00-2

Library of Congress Control Number: 2025918994

Trim: 6" x 9", Black & White interior, Paperback

Jacket design by Jonah Dempcy

Plunge Books
An imprint of Jonah Dempcy, LLC
Santa Fe, New Mexico
plungebooks.com

Printed in the United States of America

1 3 5 7 9 10 8 6 4 2

The entire universe is a great theater of mirrors, a set of hieroglyphs to decipher; everything is a sign, everything harbors and manifests mystery. The principles of contradiction, of excluded middle, and of linear causality are supplanted by those of resolution, of included middle, and of synchronicity.
—Alice A. Bailey, *Esoteric Psychology II*

The world is not a solid continent of facts sprinkled by a few lakes of uncertainties, but a vast ocean of uncertainties speckled by a few islands of calibrated and stabilized forms.
—Bruno Latour, *Reassembling the Social:*
An Introduction to Actor-Network-Theory

Courage consists in agreeing to flee rather than live tranquilly and hypocritically in false refuges. Values, morals, homelands, religions, and these private certitudes that our vanity and our complacency bestow generously on us, have many deceptive sojourns as the world arranges for those who think they are standing straight and at ease, among stable things.
—Gilles Deleuze & Félix Guattari,
Anti-Oedipus: Capitalism and Schizophrenia

Synchronistic events constitute moments in which a 'cosmic' or 'greater' meaning becomes gradually conscious in an individual; generally it is a shaking experience.
—Marie-Louise von Franz, *Psyche and Matter*

One's destination is never a place, but rather a new way of looking at things.
—Henry Miller, *Big Sur and the*
Oranges of Hieronymus Bosch

Dedication

For min älskling Lina —

The Human Design Cult

INTRODUCTION

I'M WRITING THIS BOOK to tell my story. I hope that my story can help others who have had similar experiences, both good and bad, with the Human Design System. I put off writing this book for a long time. I rationalized my negative experiences with Human Design and eventually went through something like a grieving process as I came to accept that this system I had loved so deeply was also deeply flawed. I grappled with the challenge of how to talk about the negative things I experienced. The vast majority of people I have met in the world of Human Design are kind and well-intentioned. The last thing I would want is for anyone to feel judged or rejected for their beliefs. After much deliberation, I came to the conclusion that the best thing I could do is tell my story and share what I have learned in the process of researching this book.

I first encountered Human Design in 2006. It wasn't until nine years later, in 2015, that I had my first reading and began investigating it deeply. I grappled with whether the system had any validity at all, and ultimately concluded that it did.

For the following ten years, I developed a deep understanding of the system and how it framed reality. I became a figure in the Human Design community and went on to host the world's largest Human Design conference, High Desert Human Design, in Santa Fe, New Mexico. Eventually, I became dismayed with negative aspects of the system and its effect on people, but it was difficult for me to verbalize my thoughts and feelings.

For a long time, I rejected the notion that Human Design was a cult. Over the years, I would be asked every few months, like clockwork, is Human Design a cult? I would usually answer that anything could be taken too fanatically, but no, Human Design was not a cult. It was a mystical framework, not that different from astrology. When detractors would accuse Human Design of being a cult more directly, I'd reply that they didn't get it. I dismissed them as missing the nuances of the system. I pointed to the lack of a central organization or belief system to organize the cult around and brushed off their criticisms.

Now I have come to believe that there are cultic aspects both in the Human Design System itself as well as how it is practiced in Human Design communities around the world. In some sense, Human Design is a cult, though we have to qualify that statement with a clear definition of what constitutes a cult. Does Human Design have a central set of beliefs? I'd say yes. Many in the community disagree with that statement. Is there a central organization? Yes and no. There are a few organizations that are granted official status by the lineage of Human Design practitioners originated by its founder, Ra Uru Hu, but these are the minority. Most people practicing Human Design worldwide have no connection to any official organization. Depending on how we define cult, you may see Human Design as more of a new mysticism, or New Age movement than a cult. However, based on my research and understanding of cults, I would actually argue that Human Design does fit the definition of cult as that term is commonly used.

I went through stages of grief as I slowly accepted the cultic aspects of this knowledge that I had come to love. I bargained. I rationalized. I did everything I could to try to differentiate between healthy and unhealthy uses of Human Design, cultic and non-cultic aspects. Eventually, I went on a deep dive into learning about what actually defines something as a cult.

I was surprised. I had thought cults required certain levels of behavior control, which I simply did not see in Human Design. But as I looked deeper, I realized that the behavior control was there. It was self-enforced through belief systems. I then began my journey of learning deeply about beliefs, a topic that I had previously studied through the lens of philosophy, psychology, and critical theory.

I entered into a period of inner reflection and grieving. I was no longer in love with this system. I was also no longer in love with my identity, which had become entirely reframed through it. From that point, I began exploring what I could do.

At first, I thought I could formulate a version of Human Design void of the problems I had found. This proved untenable. Next, I thought I could leave it in its entirety, but that felt just as extreme. I came to a conclusion that felt right to me. I would present my journey to those in the Human Design community, as well as outsiders who are curious to learn more about Human Design. Over the years, I was approached by people who were confused about their loved ones' adherence to the system and involvement in the Human Design community. This book is as much for them as for those who have gone deep within the system.

I resolved to present my findings on cultic tendencies in Human Design. I would present on this topic at the High Desert

Human Design Conference and I would write a book telling my story.

I went through a number of inner struggles determining how to proceed. I had been fanatically following Human Design and didn't want to become just as fanatical in my rejection of it. I also came to realize that my personal beliefs in the system were likely much stronger and more fanatical than the beliefs of the majority of others practicing Human Design. I concluded that the best way forward was to tell my story. I would share how I first came to believe the precepts of the Human Design System and later became skeptical of its validity.

In my research, I also learned a lot about belief and discovered many fascinating things about cognitive biases and the power of belief to affect our reality. I found a reciprocal relationship between beliefs and reality. It isn't a one way street. I came to appreciate that our beliefs affect our perception of reality while our perception of reality also affects our beliefs. Sometimes this two way street breaks down, and we get stuck in beliefs that are impervious to being changed or updated by reality. We stop reality testing. This, I believe, is what has happened to many of us in Human Design who have effectively shut down our critical thinking skills through thought-terminating clichés like *that's just the mind making up stories, that's only mental interference,* and many other ways of preventing actual critical thought from emerging.

I also returned to my first love, the work of Carl Jung, particularly his notion of synchronicity. Jung's work on synchronicity had a big impact on me as a teenager and young adult. I was fascinated by the mysteries of life, and it seemed Jung had discovered a key. Outside of the materialist view of reality which is so preoccupied with cause and effect, Jung discovered a parallel mechanism, what he called an acausal connecting principle. That's a fancy way of saying that synchronicities do not have causes as we understand them, and yet they still make connections. The Human Design skeptics were right in saying that Human Design seemed valid because of confirmation bias and other cognitive biases. However, rather than proving a materialist view of reality, I came to appreciate Jung's approach even more—that reality itself is made up of two aspects: the physical reality studied by the hard sciences and the psychological reality that we subjectively experience, which is beholden to the laws of synchronicity.

It is my hope in this book to explore some of these nuanced questions. What are beliefs? What do I believe? How do my beliefs affect my experience of reality? What is the feedback mechanism between beliefs and reality? I will also be exploring cognitive biases, synchronicity, attempts at scientific validation of mystical systems such as Human Design and astrology, and what I have found in terms of Human Design's cultic and authoritarian qualities, particularly as they relate to beliefs.

It is my sincere hope that readers of this work have their beliefs both respected and challenged, opening up a space for critical thinking and frank discussion. It is not my intention to dismiss anyone's beliefs, nor to assume that I know what their beliefs actually are. I always try to find some good in even the worst of situations. Opening up these discussions seems to me to be a positive outcome. It is certainly better, to me, than the belief that I wasted 10 years of my life in a system that is entirely false. I would rather believe that my time in Human Design was a necessary step to coming to where I am now, which is a place of humility. I accept my inability to ever fully overcome limiting beliefs, as well as celebrate breaking free from what I experienced as a system of self-imposed authoritarian control on my identity, relationships, and life decisions.

You are unique, and if that is not fulfilled then something
has been lost. —Martha Graham, *Blood Memory*

Don't compromise yourself. You are all you've got.
—Janis Joplin, *1968 Interview*

People are in love with opinions and borrow them as garments.
When you strip them off, you are naked,
and in that nakedness you will find your true being.
—Rumi, *Fihi Ma Fihi* (Discourses)

CHAPTER 1: WHAT IS A CULT?

IN MY EXPLORATIONS into cultic tendencies in Human Design, I found many definitions of cults. I sought to find definitions that have both academic standing among scholars as well as legal standing. In common usage, all sorts of things are given the label cult. There are some obvious cases where people universally agree on the usage of the term cult, like the Jim Jones cult, the Peoples Temple, where 918 people died by drinking cyanide-laced Kool-Aid in Jonestown in 1974. The Manson Family also falls into this category. Then, there are new religious movements like the Rajneesh movement which open up debate over whether they are a cult or not.

In discussing cults with friends of mine, both within and outside the Human Design community, I found a number of basic rebuttals to the question of cults. One of the main rebuttals I encountered is that everything is a cult—that the term cult is meaningless because it cannot be well-founded, and any organization or system that gains a significant amount of interest is a cult. Something else I encountered is the idea that any system can have a positive, non-cultic interpretation, and that a certain level of extremist fanaticism is what makes it a cult. I've also heard it said that all culture is a cult, that belonging to any identity group is a cult, or having any sort of belief is a cult.

I don't agree with these definitions. In my investigations, I found a number of established frameworks for determining a movement's status as a cult, such as Stephen Hassan's BITE Model for Authoritarian Control and Robert Lifton's Eight Criteria for Thought Reform. These models were developed via dispassionate examination of certain qualities of new religious movements, organizations, belief systems, and practices which are widely accepted as cults or cultic.

Stephen Hassan was a former member of the Unification Church, also known as the Moonies. His experience in that group led him to identify key forms of control used by cults: behavior, information, thought, and emotional control. The Lifton model was developed by interviewing captured American servicemen in the Korean War as well as Chinese nationals who had fled their homeland. Lifton published his findings in the book *Thought Reform and the Psychology of Totalism: A Study of "Brainwashing" in China* (1961).

There are many systems and organizations where it is up for debate whether they are a cult, or what level of cultic tendencies they have. On a scale of 0 to 100, I would place Human Design overall around a 40. It's nowhere near as extreme as the Manson Family or the Peoples Temple. And yet, in my estimation, it is still around 39 more percentage points than I am comfortable with.

I also mention that cults can be movements, belief systems, practices, or organizations because it is all too easy to imagine a cult purely as an organization. The fact is that cults spring up around beliefs, and beliefs are systematized. Any model of reality can give rise to cults or even in some sense be a cult. There's an interesting distinction here because obviously to be a cult there has to be some sense of membership.

Human Design is quite loose. Unless you've been through the International Human Design School (IHDS) training, there's nothing that really defines you as a member of a Human Design organization. The organization founded by Ra Uru Hu, Jovian Archive, does not have membership, beyond the ability to create a user account on their website to purchase learning materials and use their web tools for Human Design analysis. There certainly isn't a membership roster. Thus, there are organizations within Human Design such as IHDS and Jovian Archive, but Human Design itself is not an organization. At first, this would seem to excuse Human Design from any cultic tendencies on the part of its followers. It would seem that Human Design couldn't possibly be a cult because of a lack of organization. But that's not quite the case.

Cults can revolve around beliefs. Even if every current believer stops believing, another group can spring up and adopt those beliefs. This is one of the interesting points about cults and one of the reasons why for many years I refused to entertain the notion that Human Design could possibly be a cult.

In my review of models for analyzing cults, such as the BITE and Lifton models, I found that cult analysis models tend to focus on two related areas to determine whether something is a cult, control and demand. These are similar but slightly different aspects of cults.

One of the primary indicators of cultic tendencies is the level of control that an organization places on its members or that a belief system or model of reality enforces. In the latter case, it is often the adherents to that belief who are controlling themselves. There is nobody with a cattle prod giving you electroshocks if you go against their control. It is rather the adherents to the belief

themselves who control their own thoughts, behaviors, and interpretations of reality. It is self-reinforcing.

Demand is another aspect of some, but not all cults. Some cults
have high demand masked as, for instance, volunteering, where
members will spend hours a day making calls to recruit new
members. Many cults rely on unpaid labor of their members to
achieve their goals. Overall, I see Human Design as low demand,
although some members of the community do begin mission-
based projects that place high demands on volunteer labor for
their efforts. That seems to be the exception, not the rule.

Control and demand are almost always linked, although in
some cases like Human Design I see a high level of control with
low demands being placed on adherents of the system. I see both
high control and high demand groups as potentially harmful for
members and their loved ones.

That brings up another question I've been asked while developing this research: Are cults bad? It depends on how you define
the word cult. If you define a cult as a high control or high
demand group or belief system, then yes, cults are bad. It is
negative to be controlled in your thoughts, beliefs, and actions, or
to give over your autonomy in order to meet demands of others.
It is akin to an abusive relationship. There may be some benefits,
but those benefits could be achieved in another way. The negative
repercussions far outweigh the positive.

At the end of the day, it's about how we define cults. If you're
using cult to mean any organization or group that studies esoteric
knowledge, then no, it isn't bad to belong to a group or adhere to
esoteric beliefs. There are plenty of study groups that allow for
freedom of thought and belief with a minimum amount of control
or demand.

Some level of control and demand is perfectly natural. If you
enroll in college, there's a certain level of control and demand that

is expected. Your teachers will expect that you show up to class and turn in papers. The same is true for any workplace or relationship. Control and demand are not inherently bad, but high control and high demand can lead to negative outcomes. High control and high demand groups can drive people to despair, causing psychological damage that takes years to recover from.

I'm not saying that Human Design has done this to myself or others. The truth is that I don't know if my time in Human Design harmed me in any long-term way. All I can say is that my beliefs resulted in a certain level of self-control that was unhealthy for me. Over my time in Human Design, I began placing expectations and demands on myself that were unhealthy. I am not claiming that anyone else took Human Design as strongly as I did, although I suspect they did, based on my observations of the beliefs and actions I have witnessed in others in the community.

In the coming chapters we will analyze Human Design through the lens of the BITE Model for Authoritarian Control as well as other models like the Lifton model. Then, we will get into some of the juicy questions about the validity of Human Design, attempts to prove its validity scientifically, and how belief systems like Human Design work.

Note that I call Human Design a belief system. Many who are deep in Human Design will deny the fact that it is a belief system. They will say it is an *experiment* or a model for reality. I am perfectly fine with people using other words to describe their beliefs. My only caveat is to acknowledge that it is disingenuous to ignore the very real beliefs that rise up in Human Design, particularly in the work of its founder Ra Uru Hu.

We all have beliefs. I hope that the coming chapters will help us all to interrogate our own beliefs and determine for ourselves, using our own critical thinking skills, whether our beliefs are healthy or unhealthy. Only we can determine that, and it is not my goal to convince anyone that they have unhealthy beliefs. Again, I don't know what others believe. All I know is that I believed some unhealthy things about myself and the world, and I am much happier now that I have gotten rid of those beliefs. I hope that most people who get into Human Design don't go to the extremes that I did. Perhaps this work can help each of us take stock of what it is that we believe and get clarity around whether those beliefs are helping or harming us.

Chapter 2: The BITE Model of

Authoritarian Control

The BITE Model of Authoritarian Control was developed by Stephen Hassan, a former high-ranking member of Sun Myung Moon's Unification Church. Hassan had risen to become a national leader of the Unification Church's campus organization, CARP, the Collegiate Association for the Research of Principles. During his time in the organization, he engaged in extreme practices including sleeping less than four hours per night and extensive prayer and fasting. Hassan took on extreme beliefs. He believed Richard Nixon was an archangel and reported being willing, at that time, to kill or die for Sun Myung Moon. After leaving the church, Hassan began studying cults and wrote a number of books, becoming a cult deprogrammer and developing the BITE model.

BITE stands for Behavior, Information, Thought, and Emotion. These are four domains that cults can use to manipulate and control people. One of the main factors in determining whether an organization or belief system is cultic is the level of control required. In the case of organizations, it is quite literally the level of control exerted on its members, who suffer expulsion if they rebel against these control mechanisms. In the case of a belief system, it is the level of control demanded by those beliefs. Without a formal organization, such control is either self-enforced by the believer, or by other believers who police each other.

BEHAVIOR CONTROL

Behavior control is about controlling how people act. There are certain behaviors that are approved by the group or system. If you follow these behaviors, you are accepted. Conversely, there are disapproved behaviors. Depending on the system, these behaviors can be quite simple, like shaving your head, wearing orange robes, or vegetarianism, or they can be highly complex, all the way to dozens of prescribed behaviors that require analysis and scrutiny to make sure you obey them.

From my view, most of the behavior control in Human Design is self-enforced. After learning I was a *Generator*, I began enforcing the behavioral protocols of the Generator: do not speak unless spoken to, do not start anything new, make a sound when answering yes or no questions, and other behaviors that I learned over time. There are actually dozens or even hundreds of behavioral protocols that you pick up over time. It starts small. For me, it began with the idea, don't initiate. Wait to respond. Over time, I picked up specific behavioral protocols for dozens of aspects of my *bodygraph*. I would listen to Ra's lectures to glean new behavioral protocols, hints at how I "should" live. I wanted more than anything to live according to my design. To live your design, in Human Design parlance, means to live according to the prescriptions of the system. In the language of Human Design we call this the *mechanics* of your design. Everybody has a unique blueprint called a bodygraph, determined by the time of your birth. This unique blueprint contains an almost endless amount of information about how you should live your life. The great irony is that so much of the language in Human Design is about trusting yourself, when what that really means is to trust the system to tell you how to live your life.

For this reason, the vast majority of behavior control in Human Design comes from simply following the mechanics of the bodygraph. You learn that people with *Undefined Throats* should not speak unless spoken to, that those with an *Undefined Ego* should never try to prove things, that the *Undefined Head* must learn to stop thinking so much, that the *Undefined G Center* must stop searching for things, and so on. You learn about categories within categories, and subcategories of those. It is all extremely complex. There is something called *circuitry* where certain people are designed to support and be supported, others are designed to share impersonally, others are designed to be more individualistic and immune to outside influence. It goes on and on, and can take literal years to learn all of the aspects of the system. After 10 years studying my own bodygraph, I was still finding new nuances within it.

I'm sure there is a way to interpret the bodygraph nondogmatically. I did not find it. A great many people I've spoken with claim the problem I have is with the person reading the bodygraph, not the system itself. I've had many people tell me, the trick is to use the bodygraph as a tool without getting too dogmatic about it. That sounds great in theory, but in practice, the bodygraph is supposedly telling you hundreds of things about yourself, and each of these things puts you in a particular category—and each category has a prescribed behavior that can be recognized as *living your design*, living your true self and true purpose, and another behavior that is described as the *not-self*. The not-self is the catch-all term for everything that goes against the behavioral prescriptions of the system. A Generator initiating? Not-self.

Someone who has an Undefined Throat speaking without being spoken to? Not-self.

I would say probably 95% of the behavior control in the system is self-enforced. There is very little coercion from others. For one thing, many parts of the world don't even have Human Design communities, so people getting into the system are often alone, researching and studying books and lectures online. For another, the real life communities I have been a part of have been pretty accepting about each other's engagement with the system. There are three exceptions to this, where I have actually seen a fair amount of behavior control, but by and large it is self-enforced.

The first exception is in Human Design immersions, intensive retreats where people are actually kicked out for not obeying the rules of interaction based on their *aura type*. Generators must not initiate. *Projectors* are not to interfere in any way, including even looking at others. *Reflectors* must wait a lunar cycle to make decisions and are encouraged to remain more or less invisible. *Manifestors* are given free reign to do whatever they want. This veritable caste system creates a hierarchical structure of control:

Projectors must not interfere in any way, including even looking at others;

Generators must not initiate, and wait for yes or no questions;

Reflectors must also remain basically invisible;

Manifestors are free to do whatever they want.

The rules of aura type.

These are multi-day events that give people a space where everyone observes the behavioral rules prescribed to them. If you don't observe the rules, you're kicked out. What ends up happening, and I've heard this from multiple people who mostly give highly positive reviews, is that it's difficult for the first few days but then it becomes second nature. By day four a number of people have had spontaneous epiphanies, realizing how much better life is when they surrender (another keyword in Human Design) to the mechanics of their aura type. They often end up giving glowing reviews. I've heard from Projectors who started an immersion feeling skeptical of the whole thing only to go on to become true believers. After a few days of being completely ignored, they are finally recognized and invited—more keywords in Human Design. This sense of recognition and invitation lights them up, and suddenly they are crying tears of joy, proclaiming for all to hear that the system really works. They come away from the experience with a positive sense that all they have to do in life is wait for invitations, and if they can surrender to waiting, then the recognition will eventually come.

The problem I have with this is that it basically sounds like Stockholm Syndrome. We know from studying human psychology that people who are abused often end up siding with the abuser. If you have a group dynamic where a person is shunned and then later lavished with attention or affection, it's actually a psychological manipulation technique that can produce a major effect in their psyche. This effect could be described as trauma bonding and a high level of cognitive dissonance from the confusion of being treated poorly, then treated well. They felt ostracized and now feel part of the group. I'm not saying that Human Design immersions go to this extreme, because I don't really know, having never attended one. All I can say is that, from hearing firsthand reports, something is going on which results in people sometimes having an overwhelmingly positive experience, and rather than taking it at face value, I am more than a little suspicious of it. They go through strict behavior control and then after a few days of being controlled in that way, some attendees spontaneously awaken to their mechanics, in Human Design parlance, which is a fancy way of saying they radically change their beliefs.

It is basically an intensive retreat that facilitates changing belief from skepticism to being a true believer.

That's one of the exceptions to the self-enforcement of behavior control I've found. It's not self-enforcement if they literally kick you out for going against behavioral protocols.

The second exception I've found is some level of enforcing behaviors in Human Design communities, both in person and online, which include study groups, classes, online forums, or events like the High Desert Human Design Conference. In these communities, there are subtle and not-so-subtle enforcements of behaviors through admonishment, scoffing, derision, questioning, or any manner of social cues meant to make people stay in line. If you ask a question, you'll likely be asked in return, do you have an Undefined Head? This is because the Undefined Head is a marker in the chart for people whose not-self theme is thinking about things that don't matter. There are so many formulas you learn in Human Design, laden with jargon that makes it hard for outsiders to even know what you're talking about. To translate from Human Design jargon, what this basically means is that there is a certain configuration in the chart that happens to apply to about 70% of people which states they have a tendency to think about things that don't matter. Convenient, isn't it? We can dismiss the questions of around 70% of people out there by calling them not-self and invalidating their questions as thinking about things that don't matter.

The third exception is in more formal education, and that is the direct behavior control by Human Design teachers. As a former Human Design teacher myself, this is something I am probably guilty of as well. There is so much dogma in the teachings of Ra Uru Hu that to even teach Human Design is to exert some level of behavior control over others through continually directing them back to the rules of the system. I can't tell you how many times I was asked over the years to chime in on particular situations, and my answer was always to bring things back to the basic definitions from the system. In my defense, I would usually say that in the last instance, it is up to each individual to determine what is right for them. Regardless, I would still answer most questions with quotes from Ra or references to core definitions within the system.

I have personally witnessed other Human Design teachers going much further. I have actually seen Human Design teachers weaponize charts, in the sense of using aspects of another person's chart to try to manipulate or control them, and to literally tell people they are not living their design, that their mind is interfering or that they are hopelessly lost in the not-self—all because they dared to act or think in a way that the teacher does not approve of.

Overall, I still think around 95% of behavior control in Human Design is self-enforced. But that other 5% from immersions, communities, and teachers can have a large effect on people. I suppose I also include Human Design readings in this category, although the fact they are relatively short is probably a saving grace. Most Human Design readings go from 90 minutes to 2 hours in length. The brevity of the reading makes it hard to really enforce behaviors in the other person. Some readers, however, sell 5- or 10-reading blocks, or ongoing coaching for 6 months or a year, and that seems much more dangerous to me, because then you have an ongoing relationship with someone who is basically monitoring your behaviors and telling you which behaviors are living your design and which are not-self. Ironically, these types of packages are often sold as *deconditioning*, a term which usually means giving up beliefs (and is even used by cult deprogrammers to refer to the process of leaving a cult), but in Human Design has taken on special meaning. It's quite ironic that something that it sold as deconditioning can quite literally be indoctrination.

Looking at Human Design as a whole, particularly as a belief system that is not associated with any organization, the vast majority of behavior control is self-enforced. Most of the time, there's nobody there to tell you that you're not-self or try to get you to act a certain way. Most people I've met in Human Design are not part of a Human Design community, and the majority of their experience of Human Design is through reading and learning material from Ra Uru Hu or from others who have reinterpreted his work. That material gives them a certain set of beliefs that they can experiment with, what is referred to as *entering the experiment*. Depending on your aura type, you get a prescription for your experiment. Projectors are here to find out, what happens if I wait to be invited? Generators experiment and find out, what happens if I trust only the sound I make when answering yes/no questions? What happens if I make every decision in my life based on these sounds?

The experiment also carries with it implicit beliefs. Projectors are here to be recognized and invited, so they can guide. Generators are here to wait to respond, then trust their gut response, so they can use their energy *correctly* (a with special significance in Human Design). People with a *Defined Solar Plexus* are here to wait for *emotional clarity* rather than rush decisions.

Many of these beliefs might actually be healthy. It's empowering to know you don't have to rush decisions or say yes due to peer pressure. If someone has been going through life rushing and a Human Design reading tells them they can slow down and wait, that might be really healthy for them. If they've been peer pressured into saying yes to things and Human Design gives them an excuse to start saying no, all the better. The problem arises when we get into critical thinking.

If you're really trusting yourself, that should include trusting your critical thinking skills. That creates a lot of cognitive dissonance when, for example, I was told that any questions or skepticism resulted from mental interference due to the not-self. Over the years, I thought a lot about what this not-self thing is. I finally came to the conclusion that it is a catch-all term for anything that doesn't conform to what Ra said. It doesn't get more authoritarian than that. Ra Uru Hu is the authority, and if you disagree with him, you're not-self. If you question the system, raise concerns, or trust your own intuitions over what he said, you can be accused of having mental interference, believing in stories your mind made up, and succumbing to the not-self.

In my own case, as a so-called *calm eater,* I regulated my behavior to eat only in calm places. My chart says I should only eat in a calm *environment* (or "frequency") so I followed this rule like gospel. Since sleeping alone supposedly allows the aura to clean itself at night, I chose to sleep alone for ten years. While there may be real health benefits to sleeping alone, I became so fanatical that I refused to sleep with my partner due to an indoctrinated phobia that something bad would happen. When pressed to explain what that was, I'd use loaded language like *conditioning*—I didn't want to be "conditioned" by others.

Nobody controlled my behavior directly, yet I controlled hundreds of different aspects myself. Having an Undefined Throat means my not-self theme involves trying to get attention. Over the years, people in the Human Design community criticized me subtly and not-so-subtly, saying that people who have an Undefined Throat like myself shouldn't speak so much or be so productive. I was literally told that one of the deepest forms of conditioning of the Undefined Throat is the belief that I have to create or produce things in society. I'm all for giving up indoctrinated beliefs that we have to always be productive to be of value, but in my case, I am a creative person and the advice I was getting was to stop being so creative all the time.

This highlights two important points:

Cognitive Overload: There are hundreds, if not thousands, of aspects to your Human Design chart. Even a one-hour introductory reading can create cognitive overload and increase suggestibility through sheer information volume.

Pattern Matching: People deep in Human Design develop pattern-matching skills to detect whether something accords with chart mechanics ("living your design") or violates them (not-self). These patterns can be used to bend the narrative as they see fit.

The system's complexity is dazzling. Most people who don't dive too deeply probably aren't negatively affected, but if you go deep, you may find yourself practicing hundreds of different forms of behavior control until it becomes second nature. You might find yourself, like I did, having practiced for so long that you automatically follow the rules of the system. I found myself automatically waiting to speak because I have an Undefined Throat, automatically dismissing critical thinking as mental interference, and countless other habitual reactions and thought stopping techniques that kept me locked into the system.

I'd rate Human Design as a 3 out of 10 for behavior control from others, and a 10 out of 10 for self-imposed behavior control.

INFORMATION CONTROL

Historically speaking, Human Design initially had extremely high information control. This area of control is really about the flow of information and what information people have access to. It's related to thought control, which is how we process information and what we believe. Information control includes hiding certain information about a system or group or how it is structured, as well as outright deception or lying, such as rewriting history, fabricating stories, or misrepresenting what really happened.

Ra hid information behind expensive classes, reserving it only for the elite who paid him tens of thousands of dollars. I heard of one of Ra's students who paid $50,000 to gain access to more advanced levels of information. He also misrepresented the history of Human Design by developing new additions to the system, then rewriting history to claim they were always part of the system all along. In Ra's canonical origin story for Human Design, he had a mystical encounter with a disembodied voice that he first called "the Mother" and later called simply "the Voice." Concepts like *type, profile,* and *incarnation cross* were introduced years later but presented as part of the original revelation. This is a clear example of information control. Ra could have said that he was adding new developments to the system but instead claimed, against all evidence, that these were aspects of the system from the very beginning.

Ra would also shun and expel people who offered alternative viewpoints on his system. If he had a student who went on to develop their own interpretations, he would shun them completely for their supposed betrayal. The same goes for his early business partners who disagreed with changes he made to the system.

Some Human Design organizations also have a bad track record for information control by engaging in lawsuits over copyright in an attempt to prevent publication of books about the Human Design System, rather than to protect a creative work. An Italian court, the Court of Florence, ruled on June 3, 2020, that there cannot be a copyright of Human Design because it is a system, and systems cannot be copyrighted. Still, the attempt to stop others from publishing their own interpretations of Human Design does not reflect well on the officially sanctioned organizations. For much of Human Design's history, I would rate it as a 10 out of 10 for information control.

Today, Human Design information is much more accessible, with many voices offering varying interpretations. I'd now rate it around 3 or 4 out of 10 for information control, though some still maintain what might be called informational purity and silence dissent. However, thanks to a number of other interpretive lenses readily available online the level of control is much lower now than it was historically. There are still some hard-liners who dismiss alternative interpretations, but the majority of people in Human Design are more open minded to different sources and interpretations.

For those who believe in the value of Human Design and wish to promote a non-cultic version of it, I would suggest that they make all Human Design information free and readily available in order to promote an honest, impartial look at the history of Human Design. I would make public the fact that Ra misrepresented the history of the system by pretending that later additions were there from the beginning. Any attempt to omit these aspects of the history of Human Design amounts to information control.

As a side note, I encountered my own struggle around information control when writing this book. I decided to present on these topics at the High Desert Human Design Conference and was upfront and open about it, announcing my subject matter on a call with speakers and publicly announcing my intentions to leave Human Design on social media. I was told by a number of members of the Human Design community to be careful about who knows of my intentions—in other words, to control the flow of information. In all cases I said, while I appreciate their concern, it is my goal to never try to control information and to encourage people to speak freely amongst each other, without fear of repercussions for sharing whatever information they wish. Once I went public with my intentions to present this information, a number of prominent Human Design speakers dropped out from the conference. I noticed that the speakers who dropped out were the most famous, for lack of a better term, and had been in Human Design the longest, all for over 20 years. This leads me to believe that younger generations of Human Design practitioners are more comfortable with criticism of the system, something which can only be positive in reducing cultic tendencies.

THOUGHT CONTROL

The "T" in BITE stands for Thought Control. This is about controlling thoughts and beliefs, or what we might call brainwashing. If you ask me, Human Design as taught by Ra is a 10 out of 10 for thought control. To me, this is clearly the strongest form of control exerted by the system.

However, I also encourage anyone studying Human Design to come to their own conclusions here. The last thing I would want to do is exert my own form of thought control over others by telling them to blindly believe what I believe, or to take my beliefs as authoritative. These are my beliefs, and I do have reasons for them, but at the end of the day they are just beliefs. I would encourage each and every one of us to question our own beliefs and come up with beliefs that we feel comfortable with, while also challenging ourselves to go out of our comfort zone as much as possible in our explorations. Both are necessary: we ought to get out of our comfort zones, but we also ultimately have to live with our beliefs, and it is only natural to settle on beliefs that feel right to us. There is a natural push and pull of beliefs where we settle in a comfortable place, only to later question our beliefs, and then come to new conclusions and settle once again.

Why do I rate Human Design 10 out of 10 for thought control? First, let me qualify that I give it that rating specifically in the form taught by Ra Uru Hu. The various offshoots by practitioners like

Chetan Parkyn, Richard Rudd, and Karen Curry Parker seem to be much more open minded and accepting of alternative interpretations.

We can measure thought control by how much a belief system has an authoritarian, dogmatic quality that cannot be argued with. The more a system defers to supposed fundamental laws of reality rather than critical reasoning, logic, or ethical arguments, the higher level of thought control it has. Systems with high thought control refuse to provide evidence and create elaborate rationalizations to invalidate conflicting views. Human Design does this in spades. It is as if Ra developed the system in an original formulation, only to spend the next 25 years making additions to the system that shore up possible criticisms. The result is an airtight system that is impervious to criticism.

It's not just the blanket rejection of criticism as not-self or mental interference. There are actually hundreds of specific defenses in Human Design against criticism. There is an elaborate mythology around Human Design's purpose in the big picture of human evolution and the development of consciousness. There is a grandiose vision of Human Design as the tip of the spear of human evolution. Ra Uru Hu claims that Human Design is the most sophisticated and accurate system to have ever existed. Depending what criticism is leveled against Human Design, it seems that Ra came up with an answer for everything. If you criticize it for being elitist, he explains that everything is a hierarchy. If you say it is too much black-and-white thinking, he explains that everything is a binary. At each step, he explains that the real, true reality is perfectly expressed through the Human Design System, and that any criticism of the system is effectively going against reality as it is. He backs up this claim by explaining that the mechanics of reality were revealed to him in their entirety in his encounter with the Voice, a mystical 8-day experience he claims to have had in Ibiza in 1987.

There are countless ways Human Design developed itself as a belief system to be impervious to criticism, to the point where all criticism can simply be scoffed at and ignored by true believers of the system. The fact that it supposedly takes seven years of deconditioning—actively practicing the self-enforced behavior control of Human Design—to even be taken seriously is itself a safeguard against any third-party review or influence. The idea that Human Design is the one true system and everything else is *seven-centered* (read: old fashioned) is another such rejection. It's not that Human Design has one blanket rejection of other systems, interpretations, or beliefs. It has hundreds of beliefs that can each be used to draw from at will. The end result is a system that is completely impervious to critical thinking.

If you don't believe me, just talk to any true believer of the system. You will find one thought-terminating cliché after another. Concepts like *fractal lines, trajectory, no choice, rightness, Projector ascendancy, the seven-centered being,* not to mention the loaded language of many common English words being used in very specific ways, gives Human Design true believers almost endless combinations of concepts at their disposal to minimize critical thinking, rationalize their own beliefs, and control the narrative.

EMOTIONAL CONTROL

Finally, there's emotional control. Like behavior control, I see Human Design as 10 out of 10 for emotional self-control, but much lower for control imposed by others.

Nobody forced me to experience emotions in particular ways, yet I exerted high self-control through emotion-stopping techniques. In the Human Design System, I possess what is called an *Undefined Solar Plexus.* This means that, theoretically, I amplify emotions from others. It is akin to being an empath who takes in the emotions of others deeply. While I no longer believe this to be true, for a long time I thought, as I was told, that the emotions I am experiencing aren't really mine. I thought that I was taking in emotions from others. If I felt a strong emotion, I imagined that it was because I had been spending time around someone who had filled me up with their emotional state. Talk about disowning emotions! The result was that I had an emotion-stopping technique I could use any time, anywhere. These aren't my emotions, so I don't have to feel them any more. Poof. Gone. That may have been helpful in cases where I was under extreme emotional duress and needed a break to regain my composure, but it can't have been healthy over years of practice.

I don't want to assume that others have experienced as strong of emotional control as I did. From conversations with many people in Human Design, it seems there is a range of emotional expression with some people practicing going deep into their emotions. Most people who spend a fair amount of time with Human Design, however, come to take on a whole new vocabulary for describing their emotions, and a whole set of unexamined beliefs around emotions. People with an Undefined Solar Plexus like me come to take on the beliefs that emotions aren't really theirs. People with *individual circuitry* get beliefs around how their feelings of melancholy ostensibly have no explanation, and that one should never try to understand why they are feeling a certain way. Supposedly, all explanations for one's emotional state are merely stories the mind makes up.

I am actually of two minds on this one. I think there is some value in not overanalyzing emotions, and I do think we make up a lot of stories about why we feel the way we do. I also think it can be quite valuable to have emotion-stopping techniques, like those used in Cognitive Behavioral Therapy (CBT). Sometimes we really are overwhelmed by emotions and having an emotion-stopping technique can be a godsend. Overall, however, I came to have all sorts of bizarre beliefs around my emotions and, while I actually think I did a good job of owning my emotions, there were certainly many occasions where I would tell myself, these aren't my emotions. Again, I was told that I have an Undefined Solar Plexus, which means that my emotions aren't mine.

For those who have a Defined Solar Plexus, their behavioral protocol is to wait for emotional clarity. This is probably good advice for everyone. The idea is that it takes time to really know how we feel about something so we shouldn't rush to conclusions. As general life advice, slowing down and allowing space for feelings to change is a great idea. The problem arises if we begin criticizing the decisions of others based on whether they have followed this rule or not. When you take these rules seriously, it becomes easy to judge others. About 50% of people have an Undefined Solar Plexus, while the other 50% have a Defined Solar Plexus. This creates an easy way to invalidate anyone's emotions:

If undefined, emotions can be dismissed as not really stemming from them but being amplified and distorted from what they picked up from others;

If defined, they can be criticized for not waiting long enough for emotional clarity and introducing chaos through impulsive actions.

I saw time and time again how people in the system controlled the narrative by dismissing someone as not-self when they expressed emotions and had an Undefined Solar Plexus, or dismissing them for not waiting long enough for emotional clarity when they had a Defined Solar Plexus. Either way, Human Design gives a perfect way to judge others while rationalizing one's own behavior. If I judged someone's actions unfavorably for whatever reason, I was armed with a set of beliefs that allowed me to condemn them mercilessly. Thankfully, I also had a more or less blanket acceptance of people being who they are, so in most cases I would not actually get too judgmental. But I saw it regularly in Human Design communities.

CONCLUSION

The BITE model provides a framework for looking at Human Design through the lens of high-control belief systems. While the system may have positive aspects and some people don't experience it as controlling, those who spend years with it are likely to find themselves subject to ever increasing self-monitoring and self-control of their behaviors, thoughts, and emotions, along with what they say (information control).

I don't want to make any assumptions about how others use the system, not least of which because one of my complaints about Human Design is how much Ra Uru Hu used fear to sell the system. I don't want to make anyone unnecessarily afraid of Human Design. I also don't know to what extent others in the system may come to believe things as fanatically as I did. I only know my own beliefs and what I witnessed.

Throughout my time in Human Design, I came to believe a lot of things that stopped me from thinking critically. I gained a lot of new phobias that I hadn't had before, like sleeping or eating around others. I also saw a lot of self-imposed control in others, and attempts to control other people. I saw many arguments among community members where each side tried to control the narrative. There would be arguments over whose version of reality is right and true, with each side calling the other not-self, and each side claiming supremacy in living their design. At the end of the day, this kind of argument did not seem to be about critical thinking or respecting each other's unique viewpoints as much as spiritual elitism, silencing dissent, and shutting out authentic communication. Ironically, much of this was done under the guise of *nine-centered communication*, supposedly a more evolved way of communicating with each other.

When I found the BITE model, I felt a sense of relief. Finally I had found someone who could put into words what I'd been experiencing for so long. The cognitive dissonance began to lift, and I was set on a journey of self-reflection that resulted in a newfound sense of freedom. I am thankful to Steven Hassan and other cult researchers for their diligent effort in putting some of these dynamics into words. These are things I had felt but never before been able to express. Many people who come to Human Design say that they finally feel seen when they receive their first reading. That was true for me as well. I can also say that I finally felt seen by the descriptions of cult control in the BITE model. In the following chapters, I will go into detail on each area of the BITE model and then review some of the other approaches to cults. I know this information has the potential to be disturbing to some of my readers. It is my sincere hope that this information can also help some of you feel seen and gain a vocabulary for describing some of your experiences in this system, as it has done for me.

If you are not the free person you want to be you must find a place to tell the truth about that. The point is not to find a reader, the point is the telling itself.
—Anne Carson, *Plainwater: Essays and Poetry*

The freedom we are looking for is never freedom from circumstances, but freedom to respond to them.
—Paul Auster, *Leviathan*

To be a good human being is to have a kind of openness to the world, an ability to trust uncertain things.
—Martha Nussbaum, *The Fragility of Goodness*

CHAPTER 3: BEHAVIOR CONTROL

BEHAVIOR CONTROL IS DEFINED as overt and covert ways of controlling a person's behavior, including how they act and what decisions they make. It is clear to me that Human Design does not have much in the way of overt methods of behavior control. Nobody stands there with a cattle prod, zapping you if you don't eat according to your prescribed dietary regimen (called *determination* or *Primary Health System* in typical jargon-heavy fashion). Nobody will shun you if you sleep *in aura* with someone else, violating the principle that "entering into the Human Design experiment," as it is called, requires sleeping alone. In fact, so much of Human Design is framed as an experiment that you yourself validate, it's hard to imagine that there can be much behavior control at all.

For some people, this may be true. There are those who learn just enough Human Design to spur reflection and no more. But there will also be those like myself who go deep into Human Design and eventually succumb to a high level of behavior control. In some ways, it is more insidious than someone standing there with a cattle prod. The insidious thing about Human Design is that you can learn to use all the language of critical thinking, free thought, and self-empowerment while at the same time perpetuating subtle forms of behavior control.

Everything is framed in terms of following your *strategy and authority*. The premise is that each of us has one, and only one correct way of making decisions. For instance, I am what's called a *Sacral Generator,* so my decision-making process is to wait to respond and to trust my *sacral response*. It sounds great in theory. When I first learned about my strategy and authority, it sounded empowering. The idea is that all decisions in my life should ultimately be determined by trusting myself, which sounds great. The problem is that Ra claims most people have never trusted themselves, ever, because they don't know who they really are. He claims that only by looking at the bodygraph can you actually, for the first time in your life, see who you really are, and what you can really trust. In my case, this means trusting the guttural sounds I make when someone asks me yes or no questions. Now I realize how disempowering it is to have to refer to a strict belief system for every single decision in my life. For many years, however, I believed that it was actually empowering. When I referenced the system, I said I was trusting myself. This is the cognitive dissonance that arises when the language of empowerment is used for control.

There is so much behavior control in Human Design but it's hard to point to, because there is a perfect defense: nobody is making you do it. You're just trusting yourself. It's the soft sell. Sleep alone if your strategy and authority decides that's correct for you. Eat according to your prescribed dietary regimen if your strategy and authority decides that's correct for you. Be in relationships with people who honor your mechanics if your strategy and authority decides that's correct for you. Trust whatever your strategy and authority decides. On top of this, there is a tenet of no choice, which basically means everything is fated and we don't have a choice in the matter. The idea is that nobody really has a choice anyway, so you either witness yourself *choicelessly* following your strategy and authority, or you witness yourself not following it. This bizarre layer adds to the cognitive dissonance. Ra tells you that you must make the right decision by following your strategy and authority, and then goes on to say that there is no such thing as choice, anyway. In all my years in Human Design, nobody has been able to reconcile these two statements. I am left to conclude that it is actually the very fact that they are irreconcilable that makes them so effective. They are effective at causing cognitive dissonance, which encourages blind acceptance. If you're considering a rational argument, you can think it through and perhaps find problems with it. But Ra doesn't present a rational argument. He presents the irrational claim that you simultaneously must make the right decision, and there's no such thing as making a decision. No choice, said the Voice.

Depending on your strategy, you get different rules to follow. Wait to respond. Wait to be invited. Inform. Wait 28 days. Again, it is all presented through soft coercion. Nobody is forcing you to. Either you find yourself choicelessly doing this, which means you're living your design, or you don't.

Everything in Human Design is about strategy and authority. This sounds well and good if you interpret strategy and authority as trusting your own judgment. It's not so great if strategy and authority is simply a shorthand for referencing Human Design. Imagine every time you say strategy and authority replacing it with what Ra says to be true. Oh, you need to make a decision? Don't forget to reference what Ra says is true. Oh, it's a little decision? It's a big decision? It doesn't matter. No matter what size of decision, from day-to-day mundane interactions all the way to huge decisions like getting married, buying a house, or choosing a career, don't forget to always reference what Ra said.

It's a little different, right? If you say, don't forget to reference your strategy and authority, it sounds positive. It sounds like Human Design is reminding us to trust ourselves. But here's the rub. Ra says, we don't know who we are and what we have trusted our entire lives is not really us. According to Ra, we can only know what's really us through referencing the system. How do we know the system is true? Because it came from Ra, and Ra had access to divine knowledge.

It's the same thing cults have done for thousands of years. One person claims to have access to the truth. Nobody else knows the truth. Everyone has to follow the leader. This is authoritarian control in a nutshell.

As mentioned, the tenet of no choice adds another layer of control. This is the subject of much debate in Human Design communities. Whatever else it may be, no choice is a great way to stop critical thinking. If someone has a question, concern, judgment, or sees a red flag in the system, you can simply say, no choice, the system isn't for you. It actually sounds pretty great on paper. Surrendering to choicelessness sounds like a good idea because what it basically means is each of us is doing what we're doing anyway, so stop trying to change people. That sounds perfectly healthy. But in practice, it's a little bit more subtle.

There is an idea in Human Design that each of us has the potential to fulfill our life purpose. It is the potential to live the true self. And yet the vast majority of people will never live their true selves. They get *lost in the maya, lost in the not-self*. They do not get to fulfill their purpose in this life.

What happens when you don't fulfill your purpose? You don't achieve the *signature* of your aura type. This is more jargon. Your signature is one of four possibilities: satisfaction, peace, success, or surprise. If you fail to achieve your signature, you end up frustrated, angry, bitter, or disappointed by life. Obviously, nobody wants to end up missing out on their life purpose. Ra creates an incredible pressure to live your life purpose and even to fulfill a larger role in the totality. He describes those who fail to live their purpose as meeting resistance, a blanket term that he claims causes premature aging and illness. Our health depends on how much we can avoid meeting resistance. Beyond that, we have a purpose in the grand scheme of things, and it is only by living our design that we get to fulfill that purpose.

This can lead to the grandiose idea that people practicing Human Design are at the avant-garde, cutting edge of humanity, and that they are doing the evolutionary work of bringing about new ways of living. Ra claims that Human Design is for the *4% of 4%*, around 1-in-625 people, or only 12 million people alive today. This select group is here to bring about the new era. He justifies this elitism by claiming everything is a hierarchy, and it's just an unavoidable fact of reality that Human Design is at the top of this hierarchy.

Ra continues by saying Human Design is for children. Throughout his work, he urges parents to raise children according to Human Design principles from birth. He envisions a future where people raised in Human Design can live their nature. The only way they can do this is by following their strategy and authority.

Even here, it's not such a bad thing if we take it as a poetic appeal to trust ourselves more, to distrust authoritarian control mechanisms of others, and to really go deep inside and discover our own sense of meaning and purpose. Unfortunately, out of the frying pan and into the fire with this one. Ra is urging us not to trust the conditioning forces of parental figures, school teachers, bosses, government officials, and other authority figures. And yet, he is reproducing authoritarian mechanisms of control. He is telling us not to trust anyone but ourselves, but defining the only way to trust ourselves as following strategy and authority, i.e. referencing behavior control patterns laid out by him.

Again, we are examining Human Design through the lens of the BITE Model of Authoritarian Control. We are on the lookout for authoritarian control mechanisms, ironically, the same authoritarianism that Ra claimed to help people become free of.

When students developed their own interpretations of Human Design, Ra excommunicated them. He justified these actions by deferring to the fact that he had exclusive access to the source of the knowledge, the Voice. It was Ra who had the encounter, him and nobody else. There's a point of contention in Human Design communities where some people make a big deal about being *true to source* while others are more open to alternative views. Over the years, Ra even developed an explanation for why he should be trusted. He claimed that Human Design represented the most accurate description of reality possible, and all other versions of reality were further down the fractal line, a concept he created to explain the deterioration of information, like in a game of telephone. From this perspective, all information from outside of Human Design is merely a copy of a copy. The further you get away from Ra, the more information deteriorates.

As I said in the last chapter, it seems to me that Ra had 25 years to patch up every last potential criticism of his system. Someone might come along and offer an alternative viewpoint, and he had an explanation for that. They were further away on the fractal line. They had a copy of a copy of the knowledge, but not the real thing, which only he possessed.

Concepts like no choice and fractal lines create a pseudo-profound effect that give us the sense that Ra had access to some deep cosmic truths that are simply beyond us. He ostensibly had deep knowledge about the inner workings of reality that he dumbed down into behavioral formulas that we could follow. Wait to respond, wait to be invited, inform, and wait 28 days.

There are so many ironies in the Human Design System. Ra tells us he's giving us a way to get free from mental decision-making while simultaneously giving us literally hundreds of patterns to analyze. He tells us he's showing us a failsafe way to make the right decision every time, and yet our behavior must be carefully scrutinized, often resulting in analysis paralysis. Ra tells us we are here to become a passenger, a watcher who doesn't interfere with the natural movement of life. It sounds great on paper. Go with the flow of life, don't push the river, become a passenger and enjoy the ride. It sounds great, and yet these statements are all somehow used to mean, monitor your behavior, control your behavior, follow the behavioral protocols laid out by the system and good things will happen.

As we will see in the chapter on thought control, some of the biggest head trips in Human Design are around how words are redefined. Words are used to mean their opposite. Becoming conditioned in Human Design, you decondition. Precisely following the behavioral formulas laid out by Ra, you live your design. Referencing the system for every decision, no matter how big or small, you trust yourself for the first time. While these uses of language fall more under thought control, there are repercussions at the behavioral level as well. For many years I closely monitored my behavior and strictly controlled how I acted and made decisions. All the while, if anyone asked me to describe what I was doing, I said I was following my strategy and authority, living my design, and trusting myself. Whenever I slipped up and failed to control my behavior, I described it as conditioning or the not-self, shrugging that I had more deconditioning to do.

Another aspect of Human Design that often strikes newcomers to the system is how much of the advice is framed in an elitist way. Either you get it or you don't. It's reverse psychology salesmanship at its finest. You don't tell people they need to buy the product. You tell them it doesn't matter if they buy it or not because it's such a good product it'll have no problem selling itself. The right customer will recognize the value, implying they are probably not worthy of having such a good product. That's basically what no choice boils down to. Either you get Human Design or it's not for you, in which case you're doomed to live the life of the not-self.

An interesting concept I discovered in my research is non-coercive coercion, also called the consent illusion. This is a subtle form of coercion that makes people feel they are in charge the whole time, that they are consenting, and that they are not being coerced. All the while, they are being subtly manipulated. Ra would actually say not to trust him, not to believe him, just to see for yourself. He framed what he was doing as merely encouraging people to live more authentically as themselves. And yet, he continually directed people back to the only truth he acknowledged, his truth. In Human Design circles, pressure is subtle, often disguised as encouragement or guidance, making it harder to resist or name.

How do we tell the difference between non-coercive coercion and true, supportive encouragement? In the first case, the goal is to control people—to control their beliefs, their thoughts, or their behaviors. While I was working on this book, I began to tell various colleagues in the Human Design community about my changing feelings about the system, and my intentions to write something of an exposé. Most people were actually encouraging, but a few times I was left with the feeling I was being manipulated. In the case of true encouragement, I would hear things like, I've felt the same way, and I'm really glad you are bringing up these important issues. In the case of soft coercion I was told things like, *what I'm hearing is that you're lost, and you don't know what to believe — just remember, Human Design is not a belief system. You don't have to believe anything. Just trust in the mechanics. Don't let the mind interfere.*

Many who practice Human Design police each other as well as policing themselves by scrutinizing and dividing every statement and action made by a person and categorizing it as either living your design or not-self. You put it in the category of living your design if it obeys the authoritarian logic Ra has laid out. You put it in the category of not-self if it goes against what he said. Critical thinking, attempts to prove or disprove, or concerns over any aspect of Human Design are regularly minimized, diminished, and rejected. There are many ways this occurs. As mentioned, one of the most common ways is supposed not-self themes of the *undefined centers*, or, more recently, the idea that even *defined centers* can be *distorted*, in Human Design terminology.

One more form of behavior control to consider is shunning. Non-conformists are excluded and shunned from official channels. For example, Richard Rudd distanced himself from Human Design and developed his own system called Gene Keys. Instead of inviting him to share his perspectives, or even his reasons for leaving Human Design, he was simply shunned. Chetan Parkyn wrote a book on Human Design changing some of the words and language. He was also shunned. Strict adherents to Human Design often say that Ra encoded particular frequencies in the words he selected for various aspects of the system and that the words should never be changed.

Behavior control can also include isolation from friends and family. I haven't seen this in Human Design communities but it does happen through self-enforced isolation. The concept of the not-self and the notion that only those in Human Design have any chance of achieving the true self leads people to sometimes distance themselves from their families. I heard one prominent Human Design teacher who advertised as a relationship coach priding herself on how many people she had "freed" from not-self relationships, by which she meant, how many couples she had broken up.

There are certainly times when ending a relationship is a healthy step in psychological development. There are even those rare cases where one must sadly distance themselves from family members. These are rarities, not the norm. For a Human Design teacher to regularly encourage people to separate from loved ones should give anyone cause for alarm. In cases of severing ties with family members, in most cases a therapeutic modality might allow them to maintain some connection with their family. Of course this is not always possible, but it is troubling to me that there are Human Design teachers out there who are giving people a locked tight, impenetrable system of self-righteousness with which to judge their family as not-self.

The solipsism effect is at work here. Group members are made to interpret all relationships solely through the system's lens, leading to feelings of disconnection from others. Having hosted many Human Design events, one of the things I've heard time and again is the great relief people feel when they are able to be around others versed in Human Design. They report a great relief because they can finally use the same shared vocabulary with others.

While this is true of any niche topic, whether you're into avant-garde dance, noise music or particle physics, there is an especially damaging aspect of this effect in Human Design because, unlike other areas of thought, Human Design is all about decision-making and how you live your life in the microtexture of everyday interactions. Because of that, people can get to a place where they feel deeply alienated through not being able to share a vocabulary or conceptual framework with others. Every moment of every day you have a vocabulary for interpreting the smallest of interactions through a special lens. It's like looking for signs everywhere. Religious extremists may scrutinize every little thing about an interaction to look for signs from God. In Human Design, you look for signs of mechanics at work, or of the *distortion* and *resistance* of the not-self. All the jargon can lead to a point of severe alienation where you can only feel connection with others who ascribe to the same belief system and vocabulary.

The Human Design System also has a strict hierarchical structure. This is another aspect of behavior control. The hierarchy exists both in the system itself in terms of Type and other hierarchical aspects of the bodygraph, as well as in the corporate structure of Human Design institutions. You can see this quite obviously in Human Design immersions which are, as mentioned, multi-day events where Projectors and Generators are discouraged from speaking and Projectors especially are discouraged from interfering in any way, including even looking at others. To anyone who thinks it's healthy to instruct others to sit down, be quiet and not even look at others, I would urge you to learn about group psychology and what effects group shunning can have, especially when followed by grand gestures of inclusion.

Yet another aspect of strict hierarchical structure is around newcomers and outsiders to the system. Behavior of newcomers is questioned as they are expected to be not-self since they have not had seven years of deconditioning yet. This is just another way to silence dissent and to diminish free thinking. Outsiders of the system are written off as not-self, and newcomers to the system who are earnestly trying to learn it are told that they won't be taken seriously for seven years. People go out of their way to talk about how long they've been in Human Design, when they entered the experiment, in part to avoid their behavior being scrutinized. This only happens in high behavior control environments. While the behavior control may be rather invisible, it is ever present. If it weren't, people wouldn't make such a big deal about how long they've been in Human Design.

A final example of hierarchy is the division between those who met Ra and those who didn't. There are more than a few Human Design teachers who proudly boast of their time knowing him. It's perfectly natural to speak fondly of an old friend (or, in some cases, lover). It's something else entirely to have a superiority complex around it. I don't want to paint a picture of everyone sycophantically looking up to the old guard as authorities. In fact, there are many who reject the old guard as being outdated or overly sycophantic toward Ra. There's a great air of suspicion around everyone, almost like McCarthyism. Again, this air of suspicion would not exist if there wasn't a high level of behavior control going on.

I realize it can be hard to see the behavior control because of how much language is put into not conditioning each other, not peer pressuring each other, and trusting ourselves. Many people in the community do actually go to measures to avoid such bad behavior. For others, the language is a smokescreen to hide extreme levels of behavior control.

Ultimately, it is behavioral self control that is the strongest. Personal decisions are redirected to the system—*oh, I want to say hi to that person. Wait a minute, I should wait to respond.* As I said before, people who have practiced living their design for a while will tell you not to worry, that it eventually becomes second nature. They are correct, but this is actually cause for concern. After you have controlled your own behavior long enough, you no longer even notice you're doing it. It becomes second nature.

Community members gently but consistently reframe experience using Human Design terms, reinforcing system loyalty and encouraging trust. The system works. Yes, it does work, but not in the way we think it works. In the sense that it functions, yes, it works. But it functions as a mode of authoritarian control, not self discovery.

Political institutions and ideologies are the warty outgrowth of the religious thinking of man, in a way responsible for the tragedy of mankind. We are slaves to our ideas and beliefs.
—U. G. Krishnamurti, *Mind is a Myth*

Language is not made to be believed but to be obeyed, and to compel obedience. [...] Language is neither informational nor communicational. It is not the communication of information but something quite different: the transmission of order-words, either from one statement to another or within each statement, insofar as each statement accomplishes an act and the act is accomplished in the statement.
—Gilles Deleuze & Félix Guattari, *A Thousand Plateaus: Capitalism and Schizophrenia*

Censor the body and you censor breath and speech at the same time. Write yourself. Your body must be heard.
—Hélène Cixous, *The Laugh of the Medusa*

CHAPTER 4: INFORMATION CONTROL

INFORMATION CONTROL IS SECRECY, deception, lying, or other ways of manipulating what information is made available. It is essentially information warfare techniques. There are many aspects of information control that we will explore, but what it mostly comes down to is controlling what people know.

It's different from behavior control, which is directly about how you should act and speak in the world. It's also different from thought control, which has more to do with beliefs, how you think, how you see the world, mental models, and controlling how things are approached. It's different from emotional control, which is an attempt to control how you feel about things, how you process emotions, emotion stopping, and ensuring that emotions are handled according to guidelines set out by the system or group.

Information control is more like traditional information warfare. It's controlling the narrative. It's controlling what's public and private, dispersing information on a need-to-know basis. Information can be used to manipulate people, like using the drip of information to keep people hooked. Only higher levels in the cult are given access to the information, and who knows what is strictly controlled.

One form of information control is historical revisionism. That is to say, those in power may make revisionist claims about the history of the development of the group or system. As each new layer of Human Design unfolded, Ra would often claim that it was part of the original transmission of his encounter with the Voice, despite never having mentioned it before.

Ra spent over 25 years releasing new information. He could have said that these were new developments that he figured out based on reflecting on the system. Instead, he controlled the narrative so that people would believe it was already in the system all along. Instead of simply adding to the system, he went back and said these things were already in the system from the begin-ning, despite all evidence to the contrary.

Another aspect of information control is the compartmental-ization of knowledge. This isn't as much of a problem now, thanks to access to a lot of Human Design information online. For many years, levels of knowledge were locked away, reserved for those who had paid tens of thousands of dollars in training fees. Obvi-ously, there is going to be some level of information control in anything that is copyrighted. You can't just distribute college text-books unless they are public domain, and very few are. I don't want to unfairly criticize Human Design for observing copyright law. But there is a difference between copyrighted creative mate-rials and maintaining a veil of secrecy around a system.

Systems cannot be copyrighted. For decades, organizations that maintained copyright in Human Design were not clear on this fact. This reached the courts in 2020, in a case where Chetan Parkyn's Italian translation of his book *Human Design: Discover the Person You Were Born to Be* (2009) reached the courts. The

Italian courts determined that systems cannot be copyrighted and allowed his book to continue being published.

Again, I don't want to unfairly target those in Human Design for enforcing copyrights. It's a separate debate whether copyright should be maintained, abolished, or somewhere in the middle. But I do see a greater than normal attempt at information control. In the case of Chetan Parkyn, the courts found that he was not using copyrighted material. He just had an alternative point of view on Human Design. The shunning of alternative perspectives on Human Design is a form of information control.

I would say that practically speaking, information control in Human Design is pretty low these days. Vast amounts of Human Design information is out there through rampant file sharing of advanced Human Design classes and open discussions in online groups. As far as attempted information control, however, I would rank Human Design as a 10 out of 10.

Everything was doled out on a need to know basis. Ra was a closed book. He did not speak openly about his knowledge. He would bring out new information that he claimed to have been sitting on or wrestling with for decades, waiting for the right time to release it. Either it was new information he had just developed, in which case he was making revisionist claims to the history of Human Design, or he was sitting on the information for decades, in which case he was using secrecy to his advantage. Either way, this is information control. These are information warfare tactics.

Going beyond this, there were cases where Ra essentially worked in secrecy to maneuver financially-beneficial arrangements for himself and his family while betraying business partners. For legal reasons, I won't name names, but it occurs to me that even my fear of sharing openly some of the stories I've heard is itself a form of information control. One such story involves the formation of an official organization for Human

Design. Ra had a habit of selling "exclusive" licensing rights to be an officially sanctioned source for Human Design education to multiple people, leading to all sorts of disputes. In one case, he had sold exclusive rights to teach Human Design in a particular geographical region, when he fell out of communication. About 6 months later, he popped back up, this time with a new organization and a new leader, having come to a new financial arrangement. In other words, he had already extracted no small sum of money from one business leader when he appeared with a new leader in charge of a new organization. To make matters worse, the first email this leader sent out was to every licensed Human Design practitioner worldwide, claiming ownership of the exclusive rights of the system and that under the new structure, every practitioner was required to pay an annual fee of around $300 for use of the information. To those who knew Ra, they said that this email, sent by the new leader, was most likely written by Ra himself. He was trying to find a new way to extract money from Human Design practitioners.

You can see the problem here. Not only had he licensed supposedly "exclusive" rights to two different people in the same jurisdiction. He had suddenly introduced what is basically a tithe to Human Design practitioners worldwide. Having just received this email after no contact with Ra for months, the original business leader was taken aback. Since she had the same list of Human Design practitioners Ra did (he had apparently used that list, in fact), the business leader immediately replied to everyone with a simple message—do not pay the fee. Not even 5 minutes later Ra emailed a two-word reply. It said only: **** you. These would be the last words communicated by Ra to his former business partner before his passing.

That story was certainly not the only case where Ra had trouble with business partners.

On July 25, 2003, Ra wrote a public letter stating his views on three of his former business partners, Zeno Dickson, Chaitanyo Taschler, and Eleanor Haspel-Portner.

To: The Human Design Community in the United States

From: Ra Uru Hu

Subject: Misrepresentation

Hello, hello,

This is the beginning of the second year of operation of Human Design America under the directorship of Mary Ann Winiger. The past year despite some turmoil has been the most successful year yet for Human Design in America. Human Design America is the only officially licensed representative of the Human Design System in the United States. I spent many years working, teaching and trying to build with others an organization that could bring the simple values of Design to anyone.

I am a 5/1 and as such, a transpersonal being. To be transpersonal is a double edged sword. Allies are not choices and given the nature of duality, they don't all turn out to be valued partners. I have been disappointed twice in my transpersonal relationships in America. Twice I trusted individuals with this knowledge only to see them abuse their privilege and responsibility. I am not designed to be a policeman. I am a teacher of awakening. Yet, I see now that my years of silence regarding these beings have only added to their boldness. They leave me no choice but to make the following public statement.

The couple, Zeno Dickson and Chaitanyo Taschler, operate a so-called IRS non profit organization based on claiming to represent Human Design in America. This is a fraud. They have in one of their mailings published their revisionist history of Design in America. I would like to set the story straight.

In 1993, I had yet to visit America and a client of mine suggested a couple he knew. I contacted them and arranged for a visit. At the time, they published a local giveaway magazine where my first visit was announced. I worked with them for five years. They claim to have started Design in America. It is simply not true. I selected them, and supported them financially in the beginning. They were very poor. I paid my own expenses to travel regularly from Europe. They took my teaching revenue and began recording my teachings to transform into products. [...]

In their recent mailing is this line, "The main shift though (since I 'drifted' away), has been to liberate our spirits, returning to a compassionate view of the world. We've learned so much, by starting with ourselves and our own truth..."

I did not 'drift away', I broke with them and moved to Sedona, Arizona and formed a family corporation, Jovian Archive to protect the knowledge. Despite what they had done, I still offered them a license to legitimize their relationship with me and Human Design. They never signed. They are heartless and unscrupulous and the greediest beings I have ever met. They are still arrogantly stealing from my family.

Eleanor Portner, who I once considered a friend, not only has put her name on my recorded material and sells it for profit but now is busy inventing new matrixes and spamming these fantasies to the legitimate Human Design community. I find this deeply misleading and vain effort to turn a simple and valuable tool into confusion just sad.

Neither party pays royalties. Both parties were long ago offered licenses for free which they refused. I have nothing to do with them. I ask you to do the same. They do not in any way represent Human Design the way it was transmitted or is taught and practiced throughout the world. They do a great disservice to anyone who in their honest search for the Human Design System has to deal with their misrepresentation.

Jovian Archive does not in any way support these individuals nor does it recognize any of their teaching. The IHDS (International Human Design Schools) does not recognize them or any of their students. Any IHDS registered professional publicly listed with these organizations has until September 1, 2003 to end their association. After this date, to protect the general public from confusion, professionals listed with these organizations will be removed from the IHDS official register of Human Design professionals.

I have been very naïve in dealing with blackmarketeers and Design frauds. There is always someone who wants to change this or that or add this or that. The woman who wanted to remove all the detriments was my favorite. In a world rife with intellectual property theft, there are always dishonorable and unscrupulous people ready to profit from someone else's life's work. The cost of my lack of response and distaste for policing has brought me to this writing. I have been patient for many years but that time is over. Personally, I am appalled at their lack of grace and humbled by the fact that they were on my fractal.

Finally, I would like to stress that the above cases are exceptions. [...] It is a pleasure for me to see a vibrant and legitimate representative of Design in America which can truly be of service to the American people. Human Design America offers a vast array of official products and services. Human Design is knowledge that deserves better than to be sidetracked by the vanity of profiteers and frauds.

Love Yourselves,

Ra Uru Hu

Ibiza, Spain

On January 25, 2019, Chaitanyo Taschler would tell his version of the story in this public dispatch:

In the summer of 1993, a friend from Switzerland visited us and he brought us our Human Design charts. They were hand drawn by Ra Uru Hu. No computer program existed at that time. Looking at the pictures of the bodygraphs, and with the explanations of the mechanics by our friend, we had an easy time to recognize ourselves in them and we were impressed.

Our friend went back to Switzerland and soon thereafter met Ra again and told him about us and the magazine we were publishing. [...] Ra called us and asked whether we would be interested in hosting him and organizing introduction lectures and a Basic and Advanced training. [...] We were interested. We worked out the schedules and reserved the spaces and started advertising in our own magazine and in other publications around New Mexico. Toward the end of November 1993, three months after our friend had left, I drove down to the airport in Albuquerque and picked Ra up. He would stay with us in our little humble house for six weeks, the first of many long stays in the following years.

We had done a good job. His first introduction lecture in Taos drew close to 60 people and I dare say that this was the biggest live audience he ever had and would ever have. We got 10 people for the Basic Training, 8 of which then continued with the Advanced Training. By the end of the year they were all certified as licensed Human Design Analysts by Ra. [...] Before he left, Ra drew up a contract and after signing it we were officially his representatives with the exclusive rights to the Human Design System in America. At Ra's request our company was called New Sun Services America.

For the next seven years we worked tirelessly to establish Human Design in America. Zeno was the organizing part, organizing readings, lectures, classes, accommodations for the students coming from all over America and even abroad, inter-

views with Ra, and so on. During Ra's frequent visits and long stays in our house, she made sure he had everything he needed, cooked for him, washed his clothes, procured his pot, welcomed his guests, and so on.

As a graphic designer and recording artist, I created teaching materials for Ra, course materials for the students, advertising for the propaganda, published newsletters and took photographs. I recorded all of his classes and made them available for sale, first on cassette tapes and later, when the technology became available, as CDs. In 1997 I also created the very first Human Design website worldwide, www.humandesignsystem. com. [...] Most of the "big" names in today's Human Design, be that the Jovian version or some "alternatives," started out with New Sun Services' classes. Names like Lynda Bunnell, Genoa Bliven, Randy Richmond, Richard Rudd, Mary Ann Winiger and Chetan Parkyn are some that come to mind. [...]

From the moment I met Ra at the airport in Albuquerque I had my reservations about his character and his guru attitude, but I went along because I wanted the Human Design information he had. [...]

In a class in spring of 1997, he came up with the Types, Authority, Strategy and Profile. That was the point when both Zeno's and my alarm bells went off loudly, because these terms did cover up the underlying mechanics almost entirely and put Ra's opinion completely in the foreground, going as far as making up rules for "proper" behavior, which made us very uncomfortable. We had not signed up to follow an authoritarian false guru, but to promote the original Human Design System, as Ra had explained it to us in the beginning.

In the following couple of years he increasingly insisted that his opinions were the divine law and truth and he came up with more and more of these terms and keynotes. So much so that the original mechanics almost entirely disappeared. Of course our discomfort and refusal to accept his opinions as truth were obvious to him and he literally ran away from us in an emotional huff at the beginning of 1999. I'll never forget him shouting at us and then running out of our house, slamming the door behind him, never to be seen again.

Legally he had no choice but to let us continue our work and so he set up his own company, Jovian Archive, and his own website and started to undermine what we had previously built together. At one point he demanded that we let him use the manuals we had created and when I insisted that all my work of the past seven years be credited, he slammed that door shut as well. Most of our former allies and supposed friends ran away with him and participated in his completely unfounded smear campaign against us in the following years.

Ra discouraged outside sources. Teachers outside of his direct transmission were portrayed as *distorted, mental, mind-based, not-self, not living their design,* and *not true to source knowledge.* There are a myriad of ways to diminish and dismiss alternative viewpoints.

Ra considered himself, and is widely considered among adherents to the system, to be the one true source of knowledge about reality and humanity. He has a direct lineage of students who teach what he said verbatim. There can be no questioning of the validity and truth of his teachings. As I've been reminded many times, he encountered the Voice. Nobody else did. How could they think they know better than the Voice? This is information control at its purest.

The effect is to shut down inquiry. There are many catchphrases that immediately shut down critical thinking. *Do you have an Open Head? Do you have an Undefined Ajna?* Another catch phrase that sounds good but serves to prevent critical thinking is to tell people to just experiment and see for themselves. Legitimate inquiries would question premises or compare frameworks. These are met with scorn and the assumption that someone in the experiment less than seven years has nothing to contribute. Inquiries are brushed off with blanket rejections.

Some of this falls into behavior and thought control as well. The information control aspect is simply that some information is effectively censored. Instead of just disagreeing with other thinkers, modalities or teachers, they are rejected as not-self and mind driven. It's one thing to discuss why you might disagree with someone. It's another to make an ad hominem attack that they are hopelessly lost in the not-self, and then to distance yourself from any potential critical inquiry through hand-waving at fractal lines, trajectory and no choice.

Deeply binaristic thinking puts people into black-and-white in-group out-group dichotomies, giving rationalizations why the out-group can be safely ignored. Heavy jargon further divides between those who know and accept the jargon, and those question it or just don't know what it means.

There is another aspect that shuts down inquiry. Complexity of charts and esoteric terminology can prevent meaningful inquiry from others and effectively shut them out due to the extreme detail involved. As with astrology, any statement about anyone can be contradicted with its opposite. One aspect indicates someone's quick and impulsive, another that they are slow and methodical. The same is true in Human Design, where the vastness of the bodygraph gives *analysts*, as they are called, a nearly endless supply of material to draw from. To make matters worse, Ra described that each element of a bodygraph can either indicate something or its opposite—so a *gate* associated with articulation, like Gate 12, can be described as "articulate—or not." This gives a perfect out for adherents of the system to maintain their belief. I remember questioning a number of statements about someone's bodygraph *activations* that did not seem to fit them at all. The answer? That everything is a binary, and I have to remember to add or not after each and every statement about a person. I replied, if that's true then the system is useless. And yet, with a certain level of mental gymnastics, it is actually quite compelling.

The way I always rationalized this idea of the binary is that it is an archetypal spectrum that will be highlighted for a person. I happen to have Gate 12 activated, so I am theoretically articulate, or not. It is also a gate known for being moody. I recognized this tendency in myself. When I'm in the mood, I'm articulate. When I'm not in the mood, I am not articulate. At the time, I felt this was something unique to me and others who have Gate 12. I later learned that around 30% of people have a given gate activated, so it's already around 1 in 3 people who this mechanic supposedly applies to. I would hear an eloquent speaker and run their body-graph to see if they have Gate 12. More often than not, they did not. This led to more mental gymnastics. I've heard it described that everyone has every gate either as an activation or a *receptor*, and so someone who is highly articulate and doesn't have Gate 12 activated could be explained as having learned how to be articulate from others who do have that gate activated. As you can see, believing in Human Design requires high levels of mental gymnastics.

In Chapters 10-13, we will approach the question of how Human Design works. Anyone who u spent some amount of time taking this system seriously will surely have found a number of resonant, congruent statements about themselves. The question is just whether any sufficiently complex system will yield an equal number of resonant, congruent statements. We will explore this topic in more detail, but suffice it to say, the complexity and jargon of the system has something to do with it.

The ambiguity of terms also turns into using slogans, catch-phrases, and jargon to describe the system. Layers upon layers of ambiguity and jargon have a subtle effect of controlling information by continually reframing discussions through the system and shutting out outsiders from any meaningful interaction.

Some of this falls under the category of thought control because it has to do with how we phrase, frame, think about and see things. The information control element is that such ambiguity and jargon prevents outsiders from engaging with the system and giving alternative viewpoints.

All information is filtered through the Human Design System. Personal histories are filtered through a Human Design lens with special significance placed on when they "met HD." Global events and histories are filtered through the Human Design lens and prophecies. Information about happenings in the world and day-to-day affairs are described through Human Design language. Again, continual reframing through a system is perhaps better described as thought control, but the information control element is that alternative sources of information are not able to be engaged with, and must first be filtered and translated.

Ra claimed that Human Design had a scientific basis in an attempt to give the impression of legitimacy. Ra correctly predicted that neutrinos have mass as early as his 1992 book *The Human Design System,* better known as the Black Book. However, Ra failed to mention that many others made these predictions going back to the 1950s. Ra glossed over a lot of details, confusing various aspects of the sciences and hand-waving them away. In Chapter 14 we will be exploring scientific claims made in the Human Design System.

Another form of information control is Ra's claim that Human Design is only for the 4% of the 4% people that are alive in the world at any given time who are *mutative.* He believed there was a vanguard of highly evolved people spearheading human evolution into the future, and that Human Design was for them. This means that even if somebody has experimented for a long time with Human Design, they can be dismissed as not part of the elite. This mirrors notions like the Jehovah's Witnesses believing only 144,000 people will get into the kingdom of heaven.

Over the years hosting the HDHD conference I have questioned where to draw the line between responsible respect of people's privacy versus information control. One year at HDHD we had an incident involving statements made by an attendee that I felt required law enforcement intervention. I actually ended up getting the FBI involved and having a Special Agent assigned to the case.

It was the last day of the 5-day event and I returned to our closing potluck around 6 PM. Our de facto bouncer Von came to me and said I was needed immediately. He had kicked out the attendee in question and broken up a would be fight between him and another attendee. What was going on? I got the scoop from Von and the parents of an 8-year-old girl who was at the event. Apparently the attendee had been actively trying to have conversations with their daughter and had made some unsettling comments about her being his "guru" and them "not understanding" the connection they had. I chimed in that I was already uncomfortable around this attendee because he had been making comments for a number of days about the topic of consent. More details emerged. He had tried to stay behind with their daughter during a walk along Santa Fe River Trail. He was sitting on the swings at a playground with her when her parents asked them to come along. She didn't want to go, and he was defending her right to stay there—with him—telling the parents to leave them alone.

I gathered more information. Apparently he was not only talking about consent in the previous days, but more specifically, about the legal age of consent. This was more than enough to ban the attendee, which I immediately did. But I wanted to make sure he didn't come back and that proper law enforcement agencies were notified. As mentioned, I reported him to the FBI and told them all the details of the event, and they assigned an agent to the case. In the meantime, we had Von keep a lookout in case the attendee returned.

I was determined to ensure the safety of conference goers. I gave everyone associated with the event instructions to call the police immediately if they saw the attendee on the premises. I made a public announcement on Facebook with a photo of him and a description of everything that happened. I also sent a mass email to everyone attending the event with his photo and a warning that this man was banned from the event, and the police should be notified immediately if he showed up, along with the entire story of what happened. That's when I was contacted by a prominent figure in the Human Design community. She wrote that I should take down the public post immediately and that I was "burning [the attendee] at the stake." She defended him saying that he was misunderstood, he had done nothing wrong, and that people got the wrong idea. She used a lot of Human Design jargon to justify why his behavior, while abnormal to the homogenized world, was actually fully in accordance with living his design. It was us who were not-self and trying to condition him, and others, to see things according to a homogenized consensus reality. I respectfully disagreed and told her I would not be silenced in my efforts to raise awareness about the events that had transpired.

I leave it up to the reader to decide whether this effort from a figure in the Human Design community constituted a respect for the need to handle such a topic with care or if it was an attempt at information control.

Schools, workshops, barracks, prisons, hospitals: the model of
disciplinary power casts its shadow over all institutions.
—Michel Foucalt, *Discipline and Punish*

All learning, all teaching is for destructive purposes. You learn
about the laws of nature to control and dominate your neighbor.
It's a game of one-upmanship. I'm not saying anything against it.
I'm just saying that's the way it is. All learning, all teachings are
war games. Winning all the time is all that you are interested in.
—U. G. Krishnamurti, *U. G. Krishnamurti: A Life*

Education as the practice of freedom—as opposed to education
as the practice of domination—requires the student and teacher
to be simultaneously co-investigators.
—Paulo Freire, *Pedagogy of the Oppressed*

CHAPTER 5: THOUGHT CONTROL

THOUGHT CONTROL IS A BIG AREA OF CONCERN for me. This really gets to the heart of my criticism of the Human Design System. In some ways, this is the form of control that Human Design has prioritized above all else. It's as if you could allocate stat points, and some cults are very high in behavior, information, or emotional control. Human Design seems to have allocated all of its control into thought control, and the other forms of control stem from that.

Thought control could also be called belief control. It is control over how we see things, how we interpret reality, and what philosophers call our ontological commitments. That's a fancy way of saying what beliefs we have. Our ontological commitments are our fundamental assumptions and beliefs about what kinds of things exist.

Studying the thought control aspects of Human Design sent me on a deep journey into studying belief. What are beliefs? How do beliefs change? How do multiple beliefs work together in a belief system, an ideology?

In the beginning of my crisis of faith, if we can call it that, I went from having the belief that Human Design encouraged healthy beliefs about reality to the opposite. I started seeing it as a dangerous ideology of interlocking beliefs that could trap people in highly negative patterns of control. I vacillated, and over time, I came to see things a little less black-and-white. Instead of seeing Human Design as a single ideology, I came to realize that there are a variety of beliefs. Not everyone in Human Design shares the same beliefs. I also came to realize that it is possible for a belief system to have both helpful and harmful beliefs.

I have now come to believe that the majority of beliefs that I adopted through the Human Design System were limiting and overall negative to my well-being. There were and are positive beliefs as well. For someone to be told that they don't have to rush to make decisions can be empowering. To be told they must wait is disempowering. As a Generator in the system, learning that I didn't have to try to force life to happen gave me a great sense of relief. But there are many, many limiting beliefs about Generators that I am all too glad to have gotten rid of.

As I have said before, I don't want to assume that other people take Human Design as seriously as I did. Most of the negative aspects of thought control I experienced are because I went so deeply into the system. I studied it incessantly and practiced it daily.

I don't want to blame the system entirely, but I also don't want to take on too much of the blame myself. Having reflected exten- sively on this point, I found that there are mechanisms of thought control in the system that were developed over a long period of time, resulting in a very difficult to crack defense against critical thinking.

When someone takes on a belief fanatically, as I did, it is reasonable to assume that the person themselves has some part to play in it. While this is true, I'd argue that the person actually has less to do with it than we might think. I've heard that someone with acute critical thinking skills and a strong self of self would never be tricked into joining a cult, becoming a blind follower of a belief system. Those types of statements are not really accurate based on what we know about how cults work.

The question of why people join cults does not have a clear answer. Some of it may be the responsibility of the person themselves, but a lot of it may be how psychological manipulation and control techniques work. Even the most intelligent, well-adjusted, healthy and skeptical person who, for all intents and purposes, seems impervious to cult influence, would probably join a cult under the right circumstances. There are many things that can increase suggestibility. It's the wrong direction to look for personality traits that would lead someone to join a cult. Instead, we should study cognitive biases, something I will be looking at in Chapter 9. No matter how smart or well-adjusted a person is, unless they have gone to great lengths to become aware of their cognitive biases, they are still susceptible to manipulation. Even becoming aware of cognitive biases does not fully depotentiate them.

One of the things we will see when we look at cognitive biases is the role that cognitive dissonance plays. It is natural to want to be free from cognitive dissonance. It's an uncomfortable feeling to have an unresolved tension caused by two conflicting beliefs, or conflicting pieces of information. For instance, a person may be highly intelligent, empathic, well-adjusted, and have any number of other positive qualities, and still be in a cult. That creates cognitive dissonance, so it's only natural to come up with new explanations—perhaps they are faking it, perhaps they're not really so well-adjusted after all, perhaps they're not as smart as they seem, or perhaps they have a weak sense of self. I've even heard the explanation that they secretly wish to be controlled. I don't think any of these explanations are true. In fact, it's rather offensive to say that people who are sometimes suffering high levels of control, manipulation, and abuse, are secretly seeking it out. It's very much a theme of victim blaming, the belief that victims are asking for it.

I think the reason such explanations catch on is because it resolves the cognitive dissonance when confronted with ambiguity. Good people do bad things, bad people do good things, and smart people get tricked. In all of these cases, black-and-white thinking resolves the cognitive dissonance—albeit introducing more problems down the line. But it is precisely this cognitive dissonance and the ensuing collapse into black-and-white thinking that allows thought control to function.

What is thought control? It is manipulating and influencing perception of reality to ensure internal enforcement of beliefs. This is what is commonly known as brainwashing. It's not just getting people to believe things. It is manipulating the way they actually perceive reality so that their very perception of reality acts as a reinforcement of those beliefs.

If you get people to believe things, then they might believe something else later. Thought control goes much deeper. It is getting people to see reality in a certain way that continually reinforces those beliefs, trapping them in a belief system that they are unable to escape.

The only way you can do this is by completely shutting down critical thinking and getting people to use habitual thought-stopping techniques any time their thinking veers into free thought. You must ingrain internal mechanisms within them that are triggered when they begin to experience cognitive dissonance. What Ra says is true, so if someone starts to introduce contrary information, a tripwire goes off and a thought-terminating cliché fires.

No choice, not my fractal, it's all a binary, or any of dozens of clichés that can be used to terminate that thought process.

An internal mechanism triggers that essentially redirect them back to the system. It is all about redirecting any thought back to the system by having an answer for everything, creating an insurmountable wall that traps people inside, often for their entire lives.

My beliefs changed little by little and then all at once. After 10 years experimenting with the knowledge, as it is called, I finally reached a breaking point. Following a series of conversations with key figures in Human Design, my despair mounted. Finally, it culminated in an hour long conversation where my heart sank. When I brought up my emotions, I was told it was my mind interfering. I protested that it was my conscience and my emotions, to which I was told that, since I have an Undefined Solar Plexus, I should not trust my emotions. I was advised to use emotion-stopping techniques, something we will look at when we get to in the next chapter.

I spent about three weeks in a deep state of sadness and confusion. I wondered if it was all mental interference, as I had been told. Finally, I came to the conclusion that there was nothing mental about it. I was feeling uncomfortable with what I had witnessed and with what my own conscience told me. I was trusting myself, just as I'd paid lip service to all these years, but instead of trusting myself being code for referencing the system, I was trusting my intuition, my critical thinking skills, and my conscience.

After weeks of despair, the clouds lifted and I finally emerged with a newfound sense of freedom. I felt free from the limiting beliefs of Human Design. Those three weeks were years in the making. Most of the build up to my experience was invisible to me. I would feel uncomfortable about something—cognitive dissonance—but then I would resolve that dissonance by going back to safe, comfortable, black-and-white thinking. Eventually, something in me changed, and I could no longer continue on with thought- and emotion-stopping techniques. I let myself think. I let myself feel. What I thought and felt was not pretty, nor was it comfortable, but I persevered. Any birth into new awareness necessarily has a certain amount of pain. There is no increase of consciousness without some painful realizations. In my case, I realized, much to my disappointment with myself, how many assumptions I had adopted which were not only untrue, but harmful to myself and others.

Part of the issue is that we don't necessarily see our assumptions. We use our assumptions to see things. We don't directly know our beliefs. We use our beliefs to know things. I didn't know what I believed, nor did I realize what assumptions I had about the world. My eventual break with Human Design was the first time I actually saw what my beliefs were with some level of clarity.

For multiple years until I had my break with Human Design, I felt uneasy with certain aspects of the system, and yet I would rationalize, bargain, and do whatever I could to save my love for Human Design. I was so deeply invested in the system and my beliefs were so strong and unconscious that I couldn't imagine a world where Human Design wasn't real.

I had a thought experiment: what if the mechanics of reality, the underlying mechanisms and truth of how things work, were revealed to one man? Would anyone believe him? Probably not, I concluded. And yet those who did believe him would have an incredible gift, an incredible access to knowledge that nobody else in the world has. This belief fueled my continued interest and adherence to the Human Design System. I wanted to go as far with it as I could. Again, I didn't see my beliefs. I didn't even know I had beliefs.

Richard Tarnas, the brilliant archetypal astrologer, once made a statement in a lecture I attended that very much summarized my feelings about Human Design. He said that astrology was the laughingstock of the world, and yet this was probably for the best, because that meant that its value was reserved only for those who had eyes to see. This was exactly how I felt about Human Design. I believed Human Design was only for the 4% of the 4%, an elite, special group tasked with the continued evolution of humanity. It made sense to me that Human Design would be rejected by most people as pseudoscience or a cult, because they didn't have eyes to see. I did. This feeling of specialness sustained me for many years.

Let's look at examples of thought control in Human Design. This is how the Human Design System manipulates and influences our perception of reality. Obviously, our perception of reality can be expanded and changed, but the real question comes down to how and where a system manipulates and influences how we see reality. Where does Human Design stifle free thought? How does the Human Design System ensure continued belief in its claims?

Here I will quote some of the definitions directly from Stephen Hassan. A system is high in thought control if it requires members to internalize the group's doctrine as truth. This could be adopting the group's map of reality as reality, instilling black-and-white thinking, or deciding between good versus evil—what we call in Human Design the true self versus the not-self.

This can also organize people into us-versus-them, insiders versus outsiders: the insiders in Human Design who are gifted with living authentically, and the outsiders who are nothing more than brainwashed zombies, conditioned and homogenized, living not-self lives. I've heard people in the community call them NPCs, a term from videogames meaning Non-Player Character.

These Non-Player Characters are doomed to a life of frustration, anger, disappointment, and bitterness.

On this first point, you can see that Human Design is easily a 10 out of 10 for thought control. Perhaps the only caveat is that members are not required to internalize the group's doctrine as truth through overt control. It is rather through shunning and isolation if one disagrees. As we've explored, it's a soft sell. If you refuse to internalize the group doctrine, you're just ignored, or told that Human Design isn't for you.

The next point in Hassan's list is the change of a person's name and identity. Human Design does not involve taking a new name as, for instance, the Rajneesh movement did. Human Design does, however, involve significant changes in a person's identity.

Obviously, any system of self-discovery will lead to shifts in our own identity. Going to therapy can lead to shifts in identity as we gain new understandings. Changing our identity is not unhealthy per se. It's simply unhealthy if there is a level of control that reframes a person's identity. And that is exactly what we find in Human Design.

There are literally hundreds of new categories that you belong to, and these categories begin overtaking your identity. Instead of having an identity based on how you see yourself or an identity that naturally emerges through discussion and reflection, your identity becomes completely reframed through the system. You are no longer how you would describe yourself. Now you have a whole new set of words. You're a *quad right Mental Projector with Gate 58, Cross of Defiance*, and hundreds of other categories that you adopt.

For those just coming into Human Design, it starts small. You may learn you're a Generator or a Projector. You may learn that you're *single* or *split definition*. You come to learn a handful of categories, but as time goes on, the categories increase until your identity is reframed through a veritable smorgasbord of new terminology.

Even just having a few of these terms can lead to a pretty extensive identity reframing. I do think a lot of this depends on the person, and not everyone will experience such a severe reframing. Some people will really identify strongly with certain aspects of their design, and those will become prominent markers, ways of rejecting others. *You don't understand, you're not a Projector. You aren't respecting my mechanics because I'm emotionally defined and you expect me to answer spontaneously.*

I really think there's a range of experiences in terms of identity. Some people will adopt an entirely new identity. Others will shrug it off and take bits and pieces here and there. We shouldn't assume that those who take on a whole new identity are somehow more susceptible to cultish beliefs, or are secretly wanting to give away their power. There can be an assumption that the only people who fanatically reframe their entire identity in a system like Human Design are those who already have a weak or vulnerable identity. While it is true that many come into Human Design in a vulnerable place, we really shouldn't make assumptions here. We shouldn't assume that such a thing would never happen to us.

I've always had a strong sense of identity, and yet I reframed much of my own life through new identities I adopted: *the 5/1 Heretic Investigator on the Left Angle Cross of Healing, the single definition Generator with a completely undefined Solar Plexus.*

Another aspect of thought control is the use of loaded languages and clichés which constrict knowledge, stop critical thoughts, and reduce complexities into platitudinous buzzwords. It goes without saying that Human Design ranks highly in this regard.

The next aspect of thought control listed by Stephen Hassan is teaching thought-stopping techniques which shut down reality testing. What this means is using slogans, clichés, or reminders that serve to immediately cease further reflection. For instance: *it's just the mind, it's just a story, don't let the mind mentally interfere, just surrender to the form, surrender to the mechanics,* and other such slogans. Any time something comes up that would normally require reality testing—i.e., verifying if something is true or not—instead of checking if it is true, there are myriad ways of simply ceasing thought altogether.

As mentioned before, cults reject rational analysis, critical thinking, and constructive criticism. Again, we see this throughout the Human Design System where it is essentially impervious to outside influence, a closed system of thought that Ra spent decades fortifying against outsiders. There's an explanation for everything. There's no room for critical questions about the leader, doctrine, or policy. While questions may be encouraged in theory, in practice, they are dismissed as stemming from the not-self.

Thought control is exerted by labeling alternative belief systems as illegitimate, evil, or not useful. This one's pretty self-explanatory. Alternative belief systems are often described as seven-centered, or in a milder sense, simply "not on the fractal." There are degrees of rejection, ranging from calling them harmful, dangerous, evil, and illegitimate (not-self), to being seven-centered, which means that they came from an earlier time in history before we supposedly evolved to our current nine-centered form. The seven-centered form is described as the *killer monkey,* a form completely ruled by the mind. There is a range of dismissals depending on level of severity. Saying it is seven-centered basically means that it's from an earlier, supposedly more barbarous time in human evolution. It is mind-driven, *mindy,* or not-self, meaning that it is less evolved. The more forgiving but still dismissive approach is to write it off with *no choice* and *not on my fractal.*

This is kind of like saying different strokes for different folks. It's not as critical as calling it seven-centered or not-self, but it's still dismissive.

Finally, going through the BITE model's criteria for thought control, Hassan lists that systems and groups with a high level of thought control instill a new map of reality. This one is about as obvious as it gets. Human Design gives us what it literally calls a map of reality. There's no wishy-washiness with this one. It's a new map, plain and simple.

There are many systems which can give us new maps of reality. Going to college can give us a new way of seeing things, new viewpoints. But the extent to which this map of reality is isolated, closed to outside viewpoints, and so excessively detailed that it becomes its own self-referential closed system shows a high degree of thought control.

The new map is so full of loaded language that it completely replaces conventional psychological, philosophical, or spiritual vocabularies. Even highly specific language from those fields can still be explained to the layperson. Human Design language is notoriously difficult to translate, in part because of how poorly founded the terms are. One term that I never used in my years in Human Design is *correctness*. That was an idea that I just never got. But over the years, I would encounter again and again people who claim that everything in Human Design boils down to what is "correct" versus what is not-self. I was left with the impression that they meant something else entirely by that word, *correct*, than what I would mean if I used the same word. I just didn't see the world in those terms. Of course, when I would complain, my personal insights or contradictions would be reframed as the mind talking or expressions of not-self.

When I began questioning my beliefs, one of the first things I did was talk about it. I didn't keep anything private. I must have had 30 or 40 conversations about my apprehensions around Human Design. At first, I was a little scared to be so forthcoming, but I reminded myself that it would be hypocritical for me to try to control information about myself. I wanted to interrogate the beliefs of myself and others in the system. As mentioned, when I would bring up the idea that Human Design is a belief system, I heard the same thing again and again: "HD is not a belief system." I was left to conclude that, by Ra's design, the system presents itself as mechanically objective. Its premises are treated as metaphysical absolutes. This is why I brought up the philosophical concept of ontological commitments earlier. An ontological commitment is a belief about the very nature of reality. Human Design has some pretty strange commitments in this department.

Strict adherents to the system say that they actually don't believe anything. They claim to be observing the objective mechanics of reality. Yet, when you ask them to describe reality, you get the most fantastical stories of crystals of consciousness bundling after the Big Bang, of designs of various forms including a coming form called the *rave* which will have psychic abilities far beyond our imagination, the fall of empires through shifting *global cycles*, the end of community and rise of the individual, and even an eventual form we will all evolve to called *the Eron* which will be immortal and live on one of the moons of Jupiter. At a philosophical level, there are all sorts of commitments as well— that everything is binary, that everything is hierarchical, and many other beliefs that are blindly followed without evidence. Despite this, I would hear over and over again that there are no beliefs in Human Design. I am left to conclude that statements like this are a reversal of reality, another form of cognitive dissonance, that is perhaps better understood through the colloquial term gaslighting.

Throughout my journey, I kept coming up against the core belief of the system: there is only one correct path to awakening. It is assumed that everyone is not-self before finding Human Design, and all other systems are not-self. I had a lot of fear of leaving Human Design. I was afraid that I was missing out on the one real truth, something that required a leap of faith, but had the incredible reward of taking me on my trajectory to fulfill my life purpose. Trajectory is another loaded term. It means, essentially, the path your life takes. The idea is that only by living your design, by following your strategy and authority, can you enter onto the right life path and fulfill your purpose. This instilled a great fear in me that by leaving Human Design, I was shirking my life purpose. Little by little, as I took baby steps out of the system, I began to feel an overwhelming sense of relief that everything was OK. I began to overcome my instilled phobia that I would be essentially throwing away my life by leaving Human Design.

Thought control can also utilize destabilization of independent identity. Selfhood is redefined through the chart, making prior identity structures seem invalid or obsolete. When I was leaving Human Design, I realized that I had basically forgotten what my prior identity was, before I was a 5/1 Heretic Investigator and the rest of it. My independent identity was fully destabilized to the point of being obliterated. It was terrifying and exhilarating to leave Human Design because I had lost all sense of who I was outside of the definitions of the system, but that also meant I got to begin the real process of self-discovery—not the prescriptive system of beliefs that called itself self-discovery. When a system tells you who you are, you can either accept it or reject it. Real self-discovery is not about accepting or rejecting. It is a process of finding out for yourself who you really are, and that is something I had avoided doing, hiding behind all the labels of the Human

Design System. I already knew who I was: a 5/1 Heretic Investigator, a single definition Sacral Generator, and all the rest.

Much of thought control has to do with language. In Human Design, there is a reinterpretation of language and a semantic distortion where ordinary words acquire loaded, idiosyncratic meanings. This makes outside communication more difficult as well as internal thought processes strained as they continually direct back to the system and to specific ways of understanding things.

We lose critical thinking skills as we come to doubt our previous approaches to understanding. I spent many years of my life studying philosophy, and once I had gotten deep enough in Human Design, I came to believe that it was all mental garbage, stories people make up with no value whatsoever. This complete blanket rejection of my own critical thinking faculties could only happen through a slow, steady, overwhelming submersion and submission—or surrender, in Human Design terminology—to a tremendous amount of idiosyncratic loaded language.

The philosopher Alain Badiou describes a process he calls suturing whereby philosophy attaches itself to other fields in order to claim its own supremacy as a privileged discourse. It's not enough for art to speak for itself. Philosophy sutures itself to art and creates the field of aesthetics. The same is true in fields such as politics, science (philosophy of science), and even love. Badiou makes the interesting claim that the field of psychology is the result of philosophy suturing itself to love and desire. In any case, this concept of suturing fits well here. From this perspective, philosophy is inherently cultic because it is battling for control of the narrative. We could actually claim that each discourse battles for supremacy in its own way. You have scientific materialists who believe it is their discourse that reigns supreme, or you have Marxists who believe everything is the result of class struggle, or psychologists who believe in a psychological and psychologizing explanation for everything. Human Design practitioners are no different. After spending enough time in Human Design, I believed it was the supreme narrative to rule them all. I came to see all other discourses as results of characteristics best described in the Human Design bodygraph. Some philosophers were more *tribal*, some *collective*, some *individual*, following Human Design's categorization schema for different types of life force energy.

I actually think adopting different categorization schemes is a great way to approach things. It is really just the use of archetypes. All categories are archetypes, and all we are saying when we put something into a category is that we are able to see it through a particular archetypal lens. In fact, it is difficult to understand anything at all without doing this. Part of understanding is creating mental models, and that requires patterns, categories, and pattern-matching which fits things into particular categories. If our goal is to understand ourselves and the world around us, we need these things. Even the creation of new concepts and new jargon is not inherently bad. Alain Badiou uses his concept of suturing to explain all sorts of things. Another French philosopher Gilles Deleuze actually claims that the entire practice of philosophy is the creation of concepts. These activities are important for developing our collective understanding of the world. We need new concepts. We just need the right concepts, ones that enrich our understanding rather than diminishing it.

One issue with using so much jargon is that any attempt to question Human Design using regular language can trigger specific jargon associations. You can hardly make a single statement about the system without someone deep in Human Design relating it to some *center, gate, line, channel,* or other aspect.

There is also the problem of the exclusivity of language. All of reality is reframed through proprietary terminology, making ordinary expressions seem inadequate or ignorant. Human Design seems like the only real, detailed vocabulary and lens for describing the world, while philosophical, psychological, sociological, and other frameworks seem hopelessly general.

Ultimately, there is a replacement of one's internal compass. Adherents to Human Design are taught to distrust their intuition, memories, and feelings, relying instead on the system. The only way to replace one's internal compass completely is to present Human Design as omniscient, and to inculcate the demand for omniscient certainty. Members are encouraged to see the system as providing certainty in all areas of life, identity, purpose, and future. It is an absolute within the maya, in Ra's terms. Indeed, for purists in the system, Human Design is the only absolute. Everything else is relative or partial. Sometimes this is phrased as the statement that the only thing that provides certainty in life is strategy and authority—i.e., seeing reality through the lens of Human Design.

Much of thought control is enforced through circular logic. One of many head trips in Human Design is realizing the circular logic where criticisms themselves are pointed to as proof of the system's validity. *The very fact you are meeting resistance shows that you are initiating, the fact you're trying to disprove Human Design shows that your Undefined Ego is still not deconditioned, and the fact you're thinking about this proves that your Undefined Head and Ajna are still not-self.* This is twisted logic. Whether you have a defined or undefined center, whether you supposedly exhibit the not-self theme or not, a rationalization can explain anything away. Endless permutations of keynotes make it easy to make up any story. It is all too easy to explain away behavior and bend the narrative to fit a particular view, dismissing other viewpoints.

As mentioned before, there is also the aspect of cognitive flooding: overexposure to new concepts causes confusion, making people more suggestible. People having their first Human Design reading often report feeling dazed after, as their head swirls with all of the keynotes and reframing of their reality. They are flooded with new information that makes them suggestible and piques their curiosity or desire to know the answer to mysteries, preying on human nature.

I experienced a loss of my ordinary self. In my case, it was a near-complete dissociation from my previous identity, relationships, and decision-making skills. When I began seriously doubting Human Design, I had a lot of cognitive dissonance around what it really meant to trust myself. How did I make decisions before? I had spent ten years making decisions according to "my" so-called strategy and authority. I had forgotten how I used to make decisions, having spent so long believing that any other way of making decisions was not-self. I believed, as many do, that I had never made a good decision before Human Design, or if I had, it was purely by accident.

I was fully dissociated from my previous identity and had forgotten how I saw myself without using the lens of Human Design. For weeks following my break with Human Design, I had internal cognitive dissonance where I would struggle to remember how I made decisions. I literally forgot how to make decisions without referencing the system.

It's something that was so automatic to me before Human Design, and yet after Human Design it became second nature to monitor and control my behavior. I would think of calling a friend and then immediately remind myself, *don't initiate, just wait to respond.* After my break with Human Design, this would occur dozens of times a day. Thankfully, I would then have the next thought that I can do whatever I want. Then the question became, what do I want? What do I really want? How do I know I really want it, and that it's not mental interference as Human Design warned me about? It was definitely a head trip.

I can relate strongly to this sense of loss of my ordinary self. Before Human Design, I was relatively ordinary. After ten years in the system, I had lost that ordinary self completely, and it took me some time to gain it back. I am probably still in that process. Instead of an authentic identity based on self-reflection and discovery, I had what might be called a pseudo-identity formation. I had developed a new identity constructed entirely from group roles, language, and beliefs. It is pseudo because it is not based on personal experience itself but rather ready-made constructs to wear. Ra even calls them costumes and roles.

Human Design can be a system of false empowerment. The system claims to empower while actually redirecting autonomy to be subject to analysis for *correctness* within the confines of the system. Trusting yourself becomes code for adhering to the system. When we say trust yourself in Human Design, because of that jargon, it actually means trust the system. Trust what Ra said. Trust what you've come to believe is true. This leads to a loss of not only pre-system identity, but language, too. Long-term members such as myself forget how to speak about themselves outside of chart-based terms. This in turn further inhibits capacity for independent decision-making. Any words I try to use to describe myself and my decision-making would trigger a cavalcade of associations within the system. It was really hard to stop seeing things through the lens of the system, and I am grateful that I was finally able to leave it behind. Even making a statement like that would likely trigger those deep in the system to ask, does Jonah have an *Undefined Spleen*? (I do.) Is he having difficulty letting go? (I was.) And yet, these questions are basically rhetorical. They do not serve to add any new deeper insight into myself or the world. They only serve to reinforce belief in the system. They assume, first and foremost, that there is such a thing as an Undefined Spleen, and secondarily, that it makes someone have difficulty letting go of things. I don't hold either of those beliefs.

I would urge any reader who is already experimenting with Human Design to try another experiment. Try living for a few days without any reference to Human Design. Any time you think about it or interpret reality through its lens, simply move on and operate as though it did not exist. It's harder than it sounds if you are deep in the system.

Finally, there's existential dependency creation. The system becomes a primary framework through which all life experiences are interpreted, generating deep reliance. If you actually try living a day without Human Design, you'll notice dozens of times each day that something reminds you of HD—that is, if you are deep in the system, like I was.

I shouldn't make assumptions here because some of these things may have been peculiar to my own psychology, but I have seen enough others who are deep in the system to know that I'm not the only one who has had these experiences.

Emotions are not just private experiences, they are learned, performed [...] We learn to manage our feelings according to the rules of propriety and the expectations of others.
—Arlie Hochschild, *The Managed Heart*

The way we have been taught to feel is often a function of domination; controlling emotions is a way of controlling bodies and hearts. —bell hooks, *All About Love*

Happiness, anger, or fear are not only felt but also managed to produce social effects—to include some and exclude others.
—Sara Ahmed, *The Cultural Politics of Emotion*

CHAPTER 6: EMOTIONAL CONTROL

IF I HAD TO RANK the forms of control of the Human Design System, I would put thought control highest. I see behavior, information, and emotional control as subordinate to thought control. If you have free thought, then you can act and feel however you want. It's only when you take on extreme beliefs that you begin to control your actions and feelings.

Speaking personally, I controlled my emotions through emotion-stopping techniques, such as telling myself that as someone with an Undefined Solar Plexus, any emotions I feel aren't really mine. I would also sometimes feel melancholic and remind myself not to try to explain or look for any reasons for my emotions. These reminders come directly from Ra. He claims that if you try to explain why you're feeling melancholy, that explanation can become a story that you tell yourself, and the melancholy will continue. I do wonder if there is some truth to this. There is power in being able to stop a feeling, or to accept it without needing to explain it.

These emotion-stopping techniques can be bad if they stifle emotions, although in all fairness, they are not always bad. As mentioned before, systems like Cognitive Behavioral Therapy (CBT) teach emotion-stopping techniques. In CBT, you learn that when you have an emotion, you have the power to immediately reframe it as a thought—I am having the thought that I am having this emotion. That reframing can create a safe distance where you can reflect on emotions without triggering reactivity or causing distress.

Emotion-stopping is only part of the picture. Overall, I think there is a fair bit of subtle emotional control in Human Design communities. How do we define emotional control? I define it as manipulating emotions and fears to keep people loyal to the system. This could be reframing emotions or redirecting emotions back to the system, or manipulating our beliefs around emotions. Our feelings can be dismissed as mental stories. We can experience an emotional narrowing, where some emotions are habitually avoided. True reflection on emotions can be reframed as simple mental interference. The emotions don't mean anything. They just need to be waited out.

There is a lot of emotional policing that goes on in Human Design communities, telling those with a Defined Solar Plexus that they haven't waited long enough or are chaotic and telling the Undefined Solar Plexus people that they are unnecessarily amplifying emotions which aren't theirs. This can invalidate their own emotional reality.

Still, I do find a lot of acceptance of difference in Human Design communities. They pay lip service to it, and you might argue that it's merely lip service when in actuality people are rejected for being different. That does happen, but there are also those who very seriously respect each other's differences. As much as I'm making the case for the cultic aspects of the Human Design System, most of the people I know in the system have actually been supportive of my continued development as a person, even when I told them I'm leaving Human Design. I don't want people to come away with a completely one-sided perspective here.

I myself have struggled to find a middle ground that allows for both good and bad aspects of Human Design to coexist within my own beliefs. When it comes to emotional control, there are some very real negatives that stem from reframing one's emotional experience through the Human Design System.

There are also quite a few indoctrinated phobias that can emerge in the system. An indoctrinated phobia is a fear that someone didn't have before coming to the system. It is essentially a learned fear. I put this under the category of emotional control because it does have to do with our emotional responses to things. Something we might have felt comfortable with before suddenly becomes uncomfortable.

The biggest example of this, personally speaking, is sleeping alone. Before Human Design, I had no fear whatsoever of sleeping in the same bed as another person. I found it an emotionally comforting experience. Once I began sleeping alone, I enjoyed it, although sometimes I missed sleeping in bed with my significant other. I told myself this was simply my conditioning. I had to wait out the deconditioning process, at which point I would no longer have the emotions of loneliness or discomfort. This mirrors how some cults isolate people from their families and help them control their emotional state to avoid longing, sadness, and missing their friends.

I don't think it's as bad as you can find in some cults. In my review of cults, I was dismayed to hear of the extremes various cults go to in order to control their members. I don't think Human Design goes to those extremes at all. It's just the case that there are subtle, sometimes mild to moderate, and sometimes more extreme forms of emotional control, just as there are other forms of control in the Human Design System.

There is really a range, and ultimately I hope each person who encounters this system will reflect using their own critical faculties and judgment to determine how much they personally feel controlled by their beliefs, or by others in the community. How much have they controlled themselves through belief in aspects of the Human Design System itself? How much have they been controlled by others, or witnessed others being controlled?

When it comes to emotional control, I have certainly, upon reflection, had many cases where I felt a certain way and dismissed my own feelings. I used Human Design terminology to justify why my feelings didn't matter, even going to the extreme of saying they aren't my feelings to begin with.

As mentioned, I have an Undefined Solar Plexus. One of the core teachings for the Undefined Solar Plexus is that your emotions are not your own. You amplify and receive emotions from others and from planetary transits. When I had undergone periods of emotional duress, I would look to people I had spent time with to help rationalize how they had influenced me or triggered my emotional state. I studied the planetary transits for clues about why I was feeling the way I was. I didn't reflect on the emotions themselves, because part of the story I was telling myself was that emotions don't mean anything. They are just feelings. They come and go. If I wait them out, I will get back to feeling neutral again. And I did. I am just no longer sure that was such a good thing.

At this level, it's not too different from astrology where people who are deep into astrology can scrutinize every aspect of their relationships and their lives through the lens of astrological compatibility and transits. It is common in astrological communities to search for reasons why you are feeling a certain way. These reasons are usually transits, but can also be aspects made with another person's chart. *You make me feel this way because your Saturn opposes my Moon.*

I'm not bothered by people using Human Design or astrology to explain things. What's troubling is if they are using mystical language to justify bad behavior and shut down any further discussion. There is a difference between explaining and explaining away. When we explain something, we put forth ways we might approach a topic. These ways are open for discussion. If someone disagrees with our explanation, or feels it leaves something out, they can say so. When we explain away something, our explanation is final. *That's the not-self—that's seven-centered.* These kinds of explanations are really nothing more than ways of ending the conversation and maintaining some level of control.

Over the course of writing this book I made a number of revisions to this chapter. In the original draft, I included a retelling of events that occurred at HDHD one year that members of the community urged me to remove. In writing this book, I was confronted with the question: am I including unnecessary gossip, or even including a story that could potentially be libelous? Is the advice I received to remove this story itself a form of information control? The first requirement for libel is that a libelous statement is false. If a statement is true, it cannot be libel. None of the statements I made were false. I also respected the privacy of this individual and removed all identifying details, even ones that I felt would add to the context of the story. However, after much reflection, I decided to remove the story in its entirety. I will summarize by saying it involved a speaker drinking heavily, using MDMA, and having sex with an attendee at an official HDHD function, and leave it at that.

Without discussing more details of the event in question, I decided to include excerpts from voice messages I received from this speaker in the following days. A few days after the event occurred, I reached out to the person in question and brought up what had happened.

The speaker replied with voice notes laced with profanity. In one, I counted over 14 expletives in two minutes. Highlights include: "**** off, Jonah. Get the **** out of my ****ing life. **** the **** off. You're so ****ing wrong, here. You don't have a ****ing clue. [...]. You're pushing me right now. It has nothing to do with me. That's a convenient ****ing excuse so **** off and happy birthday." (I received this message on the morning of my birthday.)

Continuing in the next voice note: "I'm not the only one who is having a problem with you not respecting inner authority. We're not listening to your ****ing delusional 5th line ****ing mental seven-centered trips [...]. You're not living the ****ing experiment. This isn't Human Design, dude. This isn't Human Design. This goes back to the conversation with [redacted] years ago. She said he doesn't respect my authority. You don't. You have to ****ing get a grip, dude, because you're about to lose a lot of friends and a lot of reputation. You don't believe me? I'm gonna pull everyone together and we already talked about having an intervention with you, so **** the **** off. You have to do some ****ing serious soul-searching, dude, because you are a ****ing loss."

I will leave it to the reader to decide if I am making a mountain out of a molehill, or if we ought to hold our respected figures in the Human Design community to a higher standard. We are all human, so part of me acknowledges this is just the messy side of being alive. I decided to include the partial transcript of these voice notes because of the Human Design language involved. It adds a real life example of how a prominent figure in the Human

Design community uses HD language, which I believe gives a window into how this language can be used for good or ill.

We must look beyond the surface use of language to what is going on beneath. Are we using Human Design to empower people, or are we using the language of empowerment to control and manipulate? If we do find Human Design lacking, how do we solve this?

I will end this chapter on emotional control with one final reflection. We are all emotional beings. It is perfectly natural to feel an emotional charge about things that are important to us. None of us should be ashamed of feeling our emotions, even if they are negative. When I had a falling out with this analyst, it was perfectly valid for him to feel what he felt. I know he felt angry, and I imagine he felt hurt, too. I know that I felt both hurt and anger, along with a lot of other things. What we have to realize is that there are tools available that help with understanding and owning our emotions. We can go to therapy. We can journal. We can talk things out with friends, or use anger management techniques.

I'm reminded of the meme that men will do anything to avoid going to therapy. I imagine Ra developing the Human Design System, particularly the aspects of the Solar Plexus Center, looking at his own Undefined Solar Plexus and saying—aha, now I've got it! People with an Undefined Solar Plexus aren't wired to be emotional. No, Ra. Everyone is wired to be emotional. Some people are just naturally better at owning their emotions than others. But it isn't easy for anyone. I believe Ra had an especially hard time owning his emotions and made up a lot of excuses and rationalizations to avoid doing that hard work. Unfortunately, many in the Human Design community glamorize his rather anti-emotional bent. Even in the case of so-called emotionally defined beings, Ra encourages them to wait out the wave, that their emotions are fleeting and the best we can do is to just wait for them to be over.

Some Human Design practitioners like Michael Stenbæk Litven, Teresa Brenneman and Richard Corbett, to name a few, have gone much further in their understanding of the role of emotions in our lives. Litven brings a Jungian-Hillmanian (and deeply philosophical) approach to understanding emotion, and the need to elaborate our own inner emotional world through finding corollaries in the outer world—finding music, films, videogames or activities to match our mood. I am happy to report that many figures in Human Design do not diminish the importance of emotions in our lives. Emotions are valuable feedback from our psyche, and they are not meant to only be stopped or waited out. Yes, it is healthy advice to avoid making major decisions when in an emotionally sensitive time. It is equally important, however, to listen to and trust our emotions, if we want to be psychologically complete people. If we disown our emotions, we miss out on a huge part of what it is to be human.

CHAPTER 7: OTHER MODELS OF CULTS

IN THIS CHAPTER we will look at three other approaches to determining whether an organization or belief system is cultic.

The first model we will be exploring is Robert J. Lifton's Eight Criteria for Thought Reform from his book *Thought Reform and the Psychology of Totalism* (1961). His eight criteria are: milieu control, mystical manipulation, demand for purity, confession, sacred science, loading the language, doctrine over person, and dispensing of existence. I will describe each of these briefly along with commentary on my own experiences with these aspects in the Human Design System and HD communities.

I hate to belabor the point, and I'm sure I sound like a broken record by this point, but I really have to state again that there is a great diversity of experiences one might have with Human Design. Some people are going to read about Human Design and take a few things from it, then move on with their life. Others will go deeply into the system. Then there's the question of actual groups within the world of Human Design. There are official organizations formed around teaching Human Design, replete with certifications like you might find in a degree program. There are fringe groups and offshoots of Human Design such as Richard Rudd's Gene Keys and Karen Curry Parker's Quantum Human Design (QHD). There will be a huge range of experiences across these different groups. It is hard to generalize across all of Human Design any more than we could generalize all of astrology.

For the most part, I learned Human Design independently by listening to lectures from Ra and engaging in discussion groups online. There is a big Human Design community on Facebook and I learned many of the details of the system through extensive discussions, sometimes spanning into hundreds of comments on a single thread. My Human Design education was not through official channels except insofar as Ra's lectures themselves are an official channel. I never went through a certification program.

My experience with Human Design communities is mainly with a community I myself formed. Thus, the community I belonged to had a stamp of my own way of doing things. I joked that my Human Design conference was like the Burning Man of Human Design, incorporating all manner of activities like trips to hot springs, fire dancing, happy hour pub crawls, performing plays and disco parties.

Because of this, I actually think the community I was and still am a part of is pretty open-minded. We are an interdisciplinary group of people coming from a wide range of backgrounds. Looking at the High Desert Human Design community through the lens of control, we are most certainly a low control group. We also formed an ethics committee for the conference and took complaints very seriously. When there was bad behavior on the part of a teacher or attendee, we had an independent ethics committee review the complaints and pass judgments. This only happened a few times, but in each case we took those complaints seriously and in some cases did not invite the offending party back.

Having met people in Human Design communities around the world, I don't think that our community in Santa Fe was the exception to the norm. It seems to me that most people in Human Design are open-minded, compassionate, and concerned. There are a few people who, I assume, have more self-interested agendas, but the vast majority seem to be of a high caliber of both intellectual and emotional intelligence.

But again, I want each of us to reflect on our own experiences, and also to allow for two things to be true at once. The Human Design System can have high levels of control and cultic properties, while Human Design communities can exhibit lower levels of cultic traits, simply because they have a diversity of attendees, and not everyone is so deep in Human Design.

From my perspective, the people who got really deep in Human Design were the most cultic, myself included. Since High Desert Human Design has always had an open door policy with lots of material for newcomers, it was probably not so bad in this regard. From the first year, HDHD had an interdisciplinary approach, striving to bring philosophy, sociology, psychology, and other fields into conversation with Human Design. I think we did a pretty good job keeping it less culty than it could have been. But, of course, I am highly biased, as High Desert Human Design is still near and dear to my heart.

ROBERT J. LIFTON'S EIGHT CRITERIA FOR THOUGHT REFORM

Let's review Lifton's Eight Criteria for Thought Reform and reflect on how much each of these shows up in the Human Design System as taught by Ra, and practiced in the various Human Design communities around the world.

MILIEU CONTROL

Lifton's first criterion is milieu control. This is defined as controlling information and communication within the environment.

This corresponds to Information Control in Hassan's model, for the most part, and we have covered this already quite extensively.

I will just say that in Ra's teachings and officially sanctioned channels, there seems to be a fairly high level of milieu control, as, for instance, people bringing in Gene Keys or other offshoots, are dismissed. At something like the High Desert Human Design Conference, or in the Santa Fe Human Design community, there is a low level of milieu control. At our weekly Santa Fe Human Design meetup Human Design Catalyst we would spend weeks looking at Richard Rudd's keynotes of the gates and lines. We would invite all manner of interdisciplinary approaches, having Mayan astrologers, and many other esoteric modalities well represented. There's really a range of milieu control in Human Design, from what I would call high control in more conventional channels, to low to moderate control in the communities I was involved in.

MYSTICAL MANIPULATION

Lifton's second criterion is mystical manipulation. This is really the question of whether mysticism is being presented as a mystery or used to manipulate. In some cults, events or experiences are literally orchestrated to trick members into believing something miraculous has happened. I have never seen this occur in Human Design circles. What I have seen is a certain level of mystical manipulation in the form of explaining things using Ra's divine mystical experience. I have seen explanations that defer to mysticism instead of showing any willingness to explore alternative explanations. I myself am guilty of this. I have had unusual ideas that captured my imagination. In the past, I offered up sometimes bizarre mystical explanations with elaborate reasoning, when in reality it may just be a coincidence, when in reality, it may just be a coincidence.

We will explore meaningful coincidences or synchronicities, as Jung coined the term, in Chapter 13. But I personally have been guilty of reading too much into coincidences and taking them as evidence of supernatural or paranormal confirmation. For example, when I moved to Santa Fe, I didn't know that Genoa Bliven and Lasita Shalev, the director and assistant to the director of Human Design America and essentially the highest ranking "officials" of Human Design in the country, lived there. Then, when I bought my first home, I had no idea they lived only a few blocks away from me. When I found this out, I took it as a sign that I was on the right track. Incidentally, they later became my mentors and close friends, and I am grateful for our ongoing discussions as I wrote this book.

I think it can be healthy to acknowledge synchronicities and even perhaps to allow them to be some sort of feedback, to see them as feedback from reality. We make decisions and we look for feedback from those decisions. Sometimes that feedback does come in the form of coincidences. And yet, it is important that each of us don't read too much into that or use these coincidences to justify things. We will explore this more in Chapter 13 on synchronicity.

DEMAND FOR PURITY

The third criterion from Lifton is demand for purity. The demand for purity divides the world into pure versus impure. This is very much the case in Human Design where everything is seen as living your design versus the not-self. There is the purity of the self and the impurity of the not-self. It is a strict delineation. You are either one or the other. Ra claims that following the techniques he lays out will make you live your design as the true self, i.e. will purify you. This is a claim made in many cults and new religious movements.

CONFESSION

Lifton lists confession as one of the mechanisms employed by cults. Human Design doesn't seem to use confession, except insofar as people will sometimes confess about bad decisions they made before learning to live their design. HD certainly does not reach the levels of some cults which actually blackmail people with their confessions or enforce a certain level of guilt and shame through public confession. I don't think anyone in Human Design is using confession to reform people's thinking or control them.

The closest I can find to this behavior is something kind of like confession in conversations people have about when they disobeyed their strategy and authority. They say something like, *I knew it wasn't right, but I ignored my Spleen.* Or, *I knew I didn't have clarity yet, but I went ahead and did it anyway. I knew I shouldn't initiate, but I did.* These kinds of statements are rather mild in comparison to some of the confessional techniques used by other cultic groups.

SACRED SCIENCE

The fifth criterion for thought reform is sacred science. This one happens a lot in HD communities. Ra's word is treated as sacred science. There is no questioning in Human Design. Like I said before, my thought experiment was to ask, what if one man discovered the absolute truth of reality? When I first had this thought, I framed it as a thought experiment, but over time I came to believe it as the truth. I would often pay lip service to the experiment, rather than taking Ra's words at face value. I claimed that I did not believe Ra. I said I was just seeing for myself, but unfortunately that did not deter me from believing what Ra said to the letter with unquestioning faith.

LOADING THE LANGUAGE

The sixth criteria is loading the language. This means using jargon or thought-terminating clichés with the goal of limiting critical thinking. We saw this throughout the BITE model, how preventing critical thinking is a crucial aspect of maintaining thought control. One of the primary ways of doing this is through loaded language. This means using jargon, slogans, and clichés.

A short list of Human Design clichés follows:

Trust the mechanics

No choice

Not my trajectory

Not my fractal

Surrender

Surrender to the form

Passenger consciousness

Nine-centered way of being

Don't be not-self

Mental interference

Mental stories

Are you initiating?

You could easily add dozens more to this list.

DOCTRINE OVER EXPERIENCE

The seventh criterion for thought reform in the Lifton Model is doctrine over experience. This is where personal experiences are reinterpreted to fit group ideology. Instead of looking at the uniqueness of what has happened, it is simply categorized. How ironic is it that a system which preaches differentiation can amount to hyper-categorization of everything that happens?

When I began experiencing disbelief in the Human Design System, I was surprised to notice how many times I would reference a particular category within the system throughout the day. The same thing happens in astrology and personality type circles. Perhaps any sufficiently complex system gives enough boxes that there can be a huge task of trying to figure out the best box to fit something into.

In personality type circles, this can be trying to figure out what the best explanation is for someone's behavior or the choices they made. In astrology circles, you get the same thing. I told an astrologer friend that I'm leaving Human Design and she immediately checked my transits as well as my natal chart, telling me over a dozen details about my chart and what's going on in my life right now that supposedly explains my current experience. Incidentally, in this particular case, my astrologer friend had the wrong birth date for me. When I told her my actual birth date, she quickly backpedaled and explained that many of her previous statements didn't quite fit, and she had suspected that something was amiss. I didn't believe that for a moment. She had told me wholeheartedly the astrological reasons why I did all of these things using faulty birth information. Only later when I corrected her, she changed her tune.

There are many cases of this happening in Human Design. Usually, the "wrong chart" fits just as well as the supposedly right one. In those cases, it becomes obvious that the doctrine is being privileged over personal experience.

There is a lot of suspicion of people's personal experience in Human Design circles. Some of this is justified as we should be cautious of our own personal biases and we should acknowledge that there is a lot about ourselves we aren't aware of. And yet, this suspicion can grow to massive proportions where people's self-report is taken as the not-self and the doctrine of Human Design as the only real truth.

DISPENSING OF EXISTENCE

Finally, the last element of the Lifton model is dispensing of existence. Outsiders are considered unworthy, lost, or evil. Only the group has the right to exist. This is a rather extreme formulation of certain in-group out-group dynamics that do exist in the Human Design community, although perhaps not as strongly as they do in other cultic organizations.

Nevertheless, there is a sort of feeling that the people who have access to Human Design knowledge are the ones who are really fully existing, fully living their lives on the path toward fulfillment of their purpose. Those who don't get it are lost.

MARGARET SINGER'S SIX CONDITIONS OF THOUGHT REFORM

The next model we will look at is Margaret Singer's Six Conditions of Thought Reform. This is from her book *Cults in Our Midst* (1995).

KEEP THE PERSON UNAWARE

The first condition: "Keep the person unaware that there is a program to control or change them."

It is an open question to me whether there is really a program to control or change you in Human Design. I don't imagine anyone is sitting around brainstorming new ways to control or change people. And yet, it would be disingenuous to say that studying and practicing Human Design does not lead to some level of being controlled, as we saw in the previous chapters. It would be disingenuous to say that Human Design teachers, going back to Ra himself, aren't trying to change how other people see the world or how they behave. I suppose to Ra's credit, he is rather upfront about this fact. He says repeatedly that he is trying to get people to live their design, so he says right upfront he's trying to change them. The tricky part is that he claims he is trying to get people to be truer to themselves. Throughout his teachings, Ra states repeatedly that Human Design is there to bring people to a place of self-love and to empower them to reach their fullest potential of becoming their true selves. How could there be a program to control you if all it's trying to do is to get you to be more yourself?

Human Design is presented as making you more resistant to peer pressure. Even the terminology used, deconditioning, indicates that Human Design is trying to get you to become more yourself, not someone else. It is pretty clearly the case that people in the Human Design System are not aware of any attempt to control them or change them in a negative sense. And yet, there is a real attempt to change how they see the world, to change their beliefs, to change how they think about things, and all of the elements of control that we examined in the previous chapters. For this reason, I would say Human Design does actually meet this condition. It's not like Human Design teachers are sitting around coming up with new ways to secretly control people. It has more to do with the language around helping people trust themselves more, while secretly getting them to trust themselves less—getting them to trust the system, and to distrust any decision made without referencing the system. That's where the secrecy comes in.

If someone had told me, upon entering Human Design, that I would be conditioned to distrust my own critical thinking, emotions, and intuitions, and learn to only trust something that the system tells me is the only valid way to make decisions, I would not have been interested. Instead, I was told that practicing Human Design is a way of learning to trust yourself. I'm sure this is a point a lot of people in Human Design will argue—*but Jonah, your sacral response is you!* That may be true, or it might not be true, but either way, framing something called inner authority as the only way to make decisions is still a reference to the system. I won't belabor the point, and I imagine this is contentious, but I see trusting myself as requiring no reference to a system at all. What I learned from Human Design is that I could not trust myself, because what I was calling *trusting myself* was supposedly this other thing called the not-self. That, to me, meets the condition of keeping people unaware of what is really going on while they get deeper into the system.

CONTROL TIME AND PHYSICAL ENVIRONMENT

The second condition laid out by Singer is to control time and the physical environment, especially through isolation. Because the Human Design System is really only appealing to your cognitive abilities and your beliefs, it's more like a sales pitch. Yes, Ra will prey on people's fears and emotions. Ra does this in a way that feels manipulative to me. But nobody in Human Design is actually controlling time and the physical environment, with the possible exception of immersions.

If we're talking about actual Human Design immersions or retreats, then there's absolutely control of time and the physical environment as well as isolation from the outer world. Even in that case, it is nowhere near the levels we find in more extreme cults where people live in isolation for months or years at a time. At the end of the day, I would rank Human Design pretty low for this condition.

CREATE POWERLESSNESS, FEAR, AND DEPENDENCY

The third condition Singer lays out is to create a sense of powerlessness, fear, and dependency. This one is ironic because so much of the Human Design language is about being empowered. And yet there is an element of powerlessness as well. Again and again I came up against the notion that you must surrender because you are ultimately helpless. There is a repeated philosophical affirmation that we are all powerless to change anything or do anything.

Even more so than powerlessness, however, there is an indoctrinated phobia aspect where fears are instilled in people. You can have all sorts of new fears after getting deep into Human Design. You can have a fear of not living your life purpose, fear of missing out on being part of something special, or a fear of being conditioned by others. There is quite a sense of fear around many things, including even the future, where Human Design prophecies paint a pretty grim picture.

Finally, perhaps the strangest aspect of Human Design is how it preaches independence from all external authority and absolute trust in your own authority while simultaneously instilling dependence on something outside of you. You must trust yourself, but the only way to trust yourself is by referencing the system, thus becoming dependent on the concepts of the system in order to make "correct" decisions. If you do not monitor and control your behavior, you will end up lost in the not-self. Again, I won't belabor this point. I will just say that by the end of my time in Human Design, I was entirely dependent on referencing the system throughout the day to make any decision, no matter how small. I was afraid of all sorts of things I hadn't been afraid of before. I was afraid to fall asleep around anyone else. I was afraid to eat around other people because that would violate my calm determination. I was afraid of initiating and would scrutinize my decisions to try to find assurance I had responded. More than anything, I was afraid that if I left Human Design, I would be making a terrible mistake that would almost certainly guarantee I would be unable to fulfill my life purpose. I believed that I needed Human Design to fulfill my purpose in life.

Suppress Old Behaviors and Instill New Ones

The fourth condition of thought reform in Singer's model is to suppress old behaviors and instill new ones. Much of this was covered in the chapter on behavior control. The idea is that old behaviors must be modified.

From being in Human Design for so many years, it became such second nature that I didn't even notice I was modifying my behaviors. I completely got rid of my old behaviors and became fully conditioned to behave as I thought I was supposed to. I tried not to get attention because of my Undefined Throat. If I noticed myself getting too much attention, I stopped talking so much and did what I could to shift attention back to others. I monitored myself and tried not to prove anything because of my Undefined Ego. I tried not to take my emotions too seriously. I followed a set of prescribed behaviors entirely based on my bodygraph.

My old behaviors were successfully suppressed to the point that I forgot what they even were. I'm not too precious about it because it's not like I think my old behaviors were so amazing or anything like that. In fact, I think a lot of the advice I got from the Human Design System was probably good advice for anyone. I am glad that I became aware of when I am trying to get attention, whether it has anything to do with having an Undefined Throat or not. I am glad I learned to notice when I am getting fired up trying to prove something and how to take a step back in those situations. Bringing new awareness to these dynamics was a net positive.

My question is basic: if someone else had received my reading and I got their reading, would we both receive the same benefit from our respective readings? I think so, because the positive outcomes seem to be from what is generally good advice, especially when taken as food for thought to be considered rather than as a strict ideological truth to be adhered to.

CLOSED SYSTEM OF LOGIC

The fifth condition of thought reform is to put forth a closed system of logic. Only the system has the answers. You can't find answers outside of the system. The system is logically complete, and you can trust the leader of the system as the perfect arbiter of truth. Beyond getting things straight from the leader, you can trust the group which perpetuates the message of the leader. There are no answers to be found anywhere else. Not within yourself. Not within other systems, or in critical discussion. The truth is from on high. The system is fully closed.

There is only one truth, and there is an arbiter of truth. The one truth of Human Design came from the Voice. Its arbiter was Ra. The only source of truth is the Voice, Ra, and the group which adheres to his teachings. You cannot question his truth. All you can do is repeat it verbatim, ad infinitum.

System of Rewards and Punishments

The sixth and final condition of thought reform laid out by Singer is to use a system of rewards and punishments. The idea here is to reinforce behavior and beliefs through rewarding behavior that fits the system and punishing behavior which does not. I don't see Human Design communities as being especially egregious in terms of rewards and punishments, but they do exist to a small degree. People who adhere to the system are certainly rewarded with social inclusion, and those who contradict it could arguably be punished through shunning.

It seems to me that the Human Design System (as opposed to specific communities) has no mechanism for reward or punishment built into the system. There are no financial rewards for adhering to the system, nor are there especially social benefits when studying the system in isolation. As soon as you are part of a Human Design community, there is some reward financially (if you teach Human Design or give readings) as well as social reward through the connections you make. I don't see this as significantly different from any interest group, so I would say that for the most part, Human Design does not meet this condition in Singer's system.

I myself have been the recipient of financial and social benefits. I have been financially compensated for teaching Human Design, hosting Human Design events, and giving Human Design readings. I have been socially rewarded for my standing in the community and I have received a sort of social clout and respect for my work.

This is no different than in any field. I really don't see Human Design as worse in this regard than any sufficiently specific field of thought. That being said, it is worth talking about power structures and lack of oversight in most Human Design communities.

Any position of power can be corrupted. Whenever someone has power, there is a responsibility to use that power in a way that does not exploit others. When someone achieves a certain amount of prestige by being a doctor, professor, leader, or celebrity it is as if they have mana from heaven. Jung calls this the mana personality. Many people who achieve some level of social power don't know how to handle it and end up exploiting others.

That can happen in any system, so I don't think we should single out Human Design for being particularly dangerous in this regard. However, I do think it is important for systems to remain open to outside scrutiny and for groups to remain interdisciplinary and have a certain level of oversight.

MICHAEL LANGONE'S CHARACTERISTICS OF CULTIC GROUPS

Next, we will look at the characteristics of cultic groups formulated by Michael Langone of the International Cultic Studies Association. Langone gives the following nine characteristics of cultic groups: excessive devotion, discouraging questioning, leadership dictates behavior, elitist claims, us-vs-them mentality, unaccountable leadership, ends justify means, guilt and shame control, and expected subservience.

Excessive Devotion

The group displays excessive devotion to a person, idea, or thing. In Human Design, the person is Ra, and the idea is the system of thought that he developed. The devotion is arguably excessive because of how exclusive it is. Ra exclusively had the information, and the Human Design System exclusively explains things in a way that no other system can.

Discouraging Questioning

For Langone, cultic groups are characterized by the discouragement or punishment of all questioning, doubt, and dissent. We have already gone over this point. Suffice it to say, the punishment may be subtle, but there is definitely strong discouragement of questioning fundamental tenets of Human Design.

Leadership Dictates Behavior

In cultic groups, Langone describes how the leadership dictates how members should think, act, and feel. Again, this is familiar territory from our previous forays. Ra very much dictated how we should think through his framing of reality. He directly dictated how we should act, even to the level of mundane decisions throughout the day. As we explored in the chapter on emotion control, Ra dictated ways of stopping and framing emotions so that there was some level of control exerted over how we feel.

Elitist Claims

Another aspect Langone highlights is that the cultic group is elitist, claiming a special, exalted status. So far, we are four for four. Human Design displays excessive devotion. It discourages questioning or doubt. It dictates how to think, act, or feel. And it is obviously elitist, claiming to be part of the 4% of 4%, the elite vanguard of humanity.

Us-Versus-Them Mentality

Number five in Langone's cultic characteristics, the group has a polarized us-versus-them mentality. We have already covered this one. Some communities are more openminded, but at least in Ra's original formulation of the system it was very much him and his followers versus the world.

Unaccountable Leadership

Number six, the leader is not accountable to any authorities. I don't know that Ra did much that would fall under this category, but it certainly seems he did not consider himself accountable to anyone. He questioned the entire notion of morality and used the tenet of no choice to minimize the role of human agency.

I don't know where Human Design overall falls in this category because there is a certain amount of accountability in the community through relatively open communication about the behavior of teachers and those in leadership roles. As mentioned, High Desert Human Design has had an ethics committee that made recommendations in cases of alleged misconduct, resulting in a few speakers and attendees being banned from the conference. In other cases, when evidence of misconduct was lacking, recommendations such as mediation were proposed. Beyond the formal committee, there does seem to be a fair amount of informal open discussion about leadership and the behavior of those in positions of power, so overall I would put Human Design communities as pretty healthy when it comes to holding leaders accountable. But I am not sure how much this is a recent thing, and whether there was any accountability of Ra himself or leaders in the community in the early days.

Ends Justify Means

Number seven: the group teaches or implies that its ends justify any means. I'm not sure where Human Design falls in this category either. It would seem that Ra's moral greyness teaches that if you follow your strategy and authority, that's all that matters. The end result of living your design is seen as all important and I could imagine this could be used to justify a lot of things. In practice, I don't see people using this to justify bad behavior. It seems like even if people pay lip service to following strategy and authority as the ultimate good, the vast majority of people in Human Design have a moral compass that steers them in the right direction.

GUILT AND SHAME CONTROL

Number eight: the leadership induces guilt or shame to control members. I don't see much of this in the Human Design System either. In certain offshoots like some strains of somatic Human Design teachings, there is an element of guilt and shame in accusing people of having unresolved trauma or being in trauma response mode.

I see guilt and shame control quite low in Human Design communities. It is the exception, not the norm.

EXPECTED SUBSERVIENCE

Finally, Langone lists that subservience is expected, often under threat of expulsion or harm. I don't think anyone in Human Design has been threatened with physical harm, but there is certainly a threat of financial harm resulting from expulsion. There is a real risk of being removed from the official registry of analysts for not complying with strict agreements. For instance, the International Human Design School (IHDS) has a part of their analyst agreement nicknamed "the Richard Rudd clause." It effectively states that by becoming a trained Human Design analyst you agree to teach Human Design in its original form without combining it with any other systems. I personally know an analyst of over 20 years who was written up for being in violation of this clause because his website talked about using Human Design and astrology together. It's pretty absurd that a system that itself combines so many traditions now has an artificial limit imposed on what its practitioners can and cannot use in tandem. It is literally a cut and dry case where practitioners face expulsion for diverging from official doctrine.

Overall, I would say Human Design squarely exhibits five out of the nine characteristics laid out by Langone, with the other four not really fitting or only being somewhat matched in certain cases.

Looking at these four models, it seems to me that control is the big through-line. All cultic groups or belief systems exhibit control. The other aspect that I found in my research into cults is demand. What demands are being placed on a person? This is a little different from control in that it has more to do with what is asked of the person, without necessarily exerting control in how they go about doing it.

In looking at Human Design as a whole, I have to say it seems pretty low demand to me. The system itself doesn't really make any demands. You don't have to pay tithes to an organization or anything of that nature. The Human Design community I've been a part of seems pretty laissez-faire.

At High Desert Human Design, we would always have volunteers, but made sure to be very low demand. This was not even intentional or conscious on the part of myself and the other organizers. It is simply a core belief that anyone helping out should be respected for their unique contributions and we shouldn't expect everyone to contribute in the same way. People have different abilities and I wouldn't expect people to do anything they aren't comfortable with. Instead, I would make a list of all the tasks that need done and let volunteers choose for themselves what tasks they want and what they feel is a good amount of effort to put in in exchange for a free ticket to the event.

The same is true for speakers. In 2025, my final year organizing the conference, I put together a speaker compensation package. In previous years, speakers were not compensated. However, they also had no demands placed on them. Speakers could speak remotely on Zoom or in person if they preferred. I always went to great lengths to accommodate any special needs of the speaker. We placed little to no demands on them because it intuitively felt unfair to expect anything without getting paid.

In reflecting on others in the Human Design community, I have found that the majority make low demands on others. However, there are a few exceptions. One practitioner I know put together a team of five or six people, some of whom committed literally hundreds of hours of labor in exchange for mentorship. He would demand a one year minimum commitment. This was entirely unpaid, although it could be argued that he paid them in mentorship. In all fairness, who am I to criticize a barter economy? I'm not here to police anyone else's decisions. If they think it's fair to devote a year of their life to working for someone without pay in exchange for mentorship, so be it. Maybe it is worth it for them. I'm not them, and I can't know what benefit they receive from that mentorship. All I can say is, from the outside, it looks like someone who has achieved a position of power taking advantage of that position to get free labor.

At the end of the day, I would say when it comes to control, Human Design is pretty high, especially in thought control and what we might call belief control. When it comes to demand, I don't see the Human Design System itself making any demands, and most Human Design communities are pretty low demand. But as we have seen, there is the potential for abuse of power.

I don't want to single out Human Design in this regard, because anything that gives people a sense of purpose and mission can be exploited in the same way. I'm sure there are plenty of environmentalists out there who are doing free labor because they believe in it. Human Design is no different. If you really believe in something, it is natural to want to devote time to it.

I'm not here to judge anyone who gives free labor in the furtherance of this system. My reluctance to be too judgmental here probably has something to do with the fact that I myself have devoted untold thousands of hours of free labor to furthering the Human Design System, from starting various organizations, to archiving works for posterity, hosting free weekly events, posting videos online and much else.

The truth is, I don't regret it. Nobody placed that demand on me. I did it willingly because it was something I believed in. I appreciate that others respected my belief then, just as I appreciate their respect of how my beliefs have changed now.

At the end of the day, I consider Human Design overall to be pretty low demand, with high control. It is definitely the control side of things that bothers me the most, and is a large part of the reason why I have left Human Design.

One must write one's self: one must write what one is. This writing is always a turning of suffering into something else, a play of thought, language, and desire.
—Hélène Cixous, *The Laugh of the Medusa*

Vulnerability itself is a site where ethics can emerge. From suffering and loss, we come to recognize our obligations to one another.
—Judith Butler, *Precarious Life*

If a man devotes himself to the instructions of his own unconscious, it can bestow this gift [of renewal], so that suddenly life, which has been stale and dull, turns into a rich unending inner adventure, full of creative possibilities.
—Marie-Louise von Franz, *The Process of Individuation*

CHAPTER 8: POSITIVE IMPACTS OF

HUMAN DESIGN

IT MIGHT SEEM WITH ALL THE NEGATIVITY of the previous chapters that there aren't any positive effects of studying and practicing Human Design. This is not the case. Yes, we can become trapped in limiting beliefs and negative thought patterns. But, like most systems of personal discovery, there can be a lot of benefits, too.

I have personally seen many positive effects of the Human Design System in myself and in others. I'd like to take this chapter to explore some of those effects, with the caveat that I don't believe they outweigh the negatives overall, nor do I believe that Human Design is unique in having these effects. I actually think that just about any system that encourages self-reflection will have some positive benefit.

For some reason, I have gotten to know quite a few people over the years who have been members of groups that are often considered cults. I don't say they were in cults, because that's up for debate. One of my close friends of some years, who is 76 years old at the time of this writing, was at the highest echelons of the Hare

Krishna movement, technically named ISKCON. That movement is debatably a cult. It is more commonly described as a new religious movement. It is also debatably not so new, as ISKCON is in direct lineage to the teachings of Chaitanya Mahaprabhu from the 15th century, but the organization itself did not emerge until 1966.

I have known quite a few former members of the Rajneesh Movement. In fact, many of the leading figures in Human Design are former members. Again, I have to be a little careful here because it is debatable whether the Rajneesh Movement was a cult, but it certainly fits the criteria. As mentioned, the term I see most often for describing groups like this is *new religious movement*. I would urge each of us to reflect for ourselves on whether we consider something a cult, or cultic, rather than jumping to labels. I personally see the Rajneesh Movement as a cult and I believe there is good evidence for this assertion.

I have also known many former members of Landmark Forum, originally called Erhardt Seminar Training (EST, stylized as est in all lowercase by the founder). I even met someone who grew up in an Enneagram community with extreme beliefs and high levels of control. Again, I have to be careful as I don't want to end up in a lawsuit over characterizing these groups as cults. Suffice it to say, these are groups that may or may not be cultic. Ultimately, I leave it up to the reader to analyze the potential cultic tendencies of these groups.

Through long conversations with members of these and other similar groups, I found a huge range of experience. Some people have nothing but positive things to say about their time in these groups. Others are uniformly negative. Most people are in the medium-to-positive area. I was surprised to find that many people don't experience much of a negative effect at all, or if they admit to negative effects, still find that the positives outweigh the negatives for them.

It would be too easy to claim that their self-report is flawed. It would also be hypocritical. If one of my complaints about high control groups is how much they dismiss personal experience, it would be hypocritical of me to do precisely that. It's a more challenging, and I think more honest approach to accept that there are genuine benefits as well as negatives.

I have heard attendees of Landmark give glowing reviews of how it was a transformational, life-changing event, and set them on what they consider the right path for the rest of their lives. This has even been the case when someone only attended a few sessions back in the 1970s, and thinks back fondly to how much those sessions had a healing effect on them. I heard from one woman who said she was able to fully forgive her mother and develop a deep sense of compassion after having attended Landmark, at that time called *est*.

At the same time, my own aunt attended Landmark and used what were essentially emotional blackmail and manipulation techniques to get other members of her family, including myself, to attend. Even though I was only a teenager, I knew something was fishy. I came away from the experience, which was a free three-hour introductory talk on a Friday evening, absolutely positive it was a cult. That conviction remains to this day. My experiences as a teenager attending an introductory meeting at the Seattle chapter of Landmark included meeting someone claiming to have been there for their first time who I believe was actually planted there to recruit people. I saw emotional manipulation techniques, including dim lights, hypnotic pacing, and hypnotic techniques of language, along with weirdly idiosyncratic, incorrect grammar that put people into a trance-like state. That is something that I was familiar with from studying the hypnotherapy techniques of Milton Erickson. There were also testimonials talking about highly traumatic things like accidental death and abuse that, from my view, triggered people into a state of suggestibility. Finally, there was high pressure to sign up for longer seminars. This combination of factors convinced me that Landmark was absolutely using manipulation to try to control people and enlist them to further its membership and exploit them financially.

I had another friend who was close to my age who had gone through a more extensive program with Landmark due to his mother's involvement. She had given the organization tens of thousands of dollars and volunteered long hours in recruitment campaigns calling people. She sent him to the organization for a multi-day event which included sleep deprivation, public humiliation, and confession.

And yet, even with all of this damning information, and the fact that I personally gained nothing from what was admittedly only a three-hour introductory seminar, I don't want to invalidate other people's experiences. Obviously, their testimony and self-report should be scrutinized because one of the ideas of a cult is that by essentially brainwashing people, they get all sorts of false positives in terms of the benefits for that person's life. At the same time, I don't think it's fair to simply dismiss those testimonials.

Back when I was a startup entrepreneur in the Techstars program, I was developing an idea for mentorship for executive teams. One of my mentors told me how every year or two, her company would hire some experts to come in. They would do seminars and workshops with the leadership of the company. The funny thing is, she said she didn't really care who they were, because it was all pretty much the same thing. I was surprised by this. How could that be? Her point was that, basically, any time you put an effort into something, you're going to see some results simply because of that effort. In her opinion, the modality didn't really matter. It was just the fact that you were putting energy into self-reflection that had a positive effect. You got people thinking and talking about things, and the very fact of spending effort got results. That stuck with me.

I have a similar approach to Human Design. I think for most people, it is not really harmful to learn about Human Design if they don't get too wrapped up in it. In fact, it may even be helpful if it leads them to reflect on their own lives, the decisions they've made, where they live, what they do, who they spend time with and their own attitudes about life. These are big questions and we can all benefit from reflecting on them.

With that, I'll share some of the personally beneficial effects Human Design has had on my life. These are areas where I believe learning certain aspects of Human Design got me thinking about things I didn't otherwise consider.

The first thing that really captured me was profile. The concept of profile has to do with our purpose in life and what role we play in the totality. When I began studying Human Design, I was interested in learning how the profiles worked. I began looking at the profiles of my friends. I suddenly had all these new categories to group people in. It was incredible to me how accurate it was. Although, as we will explore in later chapters, I now believe much of this was synchronicity, combined with a healthy dose of cognitive biases, including the confirmation bias.

But suffice it to say, I was incredibly impressed with the Human Design System. I found its descriptions to be deep and insightful. I would say the first benefit right off the bat was to expand the horizons of my thought and to get me to consider the roles people play in a new light.

Profile was fascinating to me. I felt empowered being a 5/1 Heretic Investigator. There were many empowering qualities about the 5/1 that I learned and came to identify with. It gave me confidence to do my best to deliver practical solutions to people.

Learning about the 5/1 also gave me more confidence to take on leadership positions.

I learned about so-called "5th line paranoia"—the idea that it can be healthy to be skeptical of what people say they expect from us. I felt deeply validated in what I had already learned from psychoanalysis: that people are unable to tell you exactly what they want from you because they do not fully know their own unconscious desire. How this looks in Human Design is the idea that people who *carry* the 5th line must be alert to the expectations others have of them—expectations that the other person may not even be aware of. That, to me, is a healthy attitude.

If I had to say what became unhealthy, it is that I believed profile determined what someone should do in their life. I'm a 5/1 in the system, so I believed that gave me marching orders for life. I believed the advice for the 5/1 profile applied to me more than to people who have other profiles. Now, I think it is more likely that the advice for all the profiles applies equally to everyone.

When people would guess my profile, they would often guess that I carry the 4th line, known in Human Design for networking, community, charity, brotherhood and sisterhood, fellowship, and friendship. Not only am I not a 4th line profile, I only have a single 4th line out of the 26 activations in my chart, which is exceedingly rare. This, and other evidence, which we will explore in Chapter 14, has basically shown to me that the bodygraph doesn't tell you what applies to you. The themes that are explored in Human Design are universal themes. They are archetypal. They apply more or less based on any number of factors of which the bodygraph does not seem to be one. They also may apply more or less at different times in a person's life. We will explore these complexities in Chapter 14 where we look at attempts to prove or disprove the Human Design System.

Over my first year studying Human Design, profile was my central point of interest, although I also began experimenting with my strategy and authority as a Sacral Generator. I began fervently tracking my not-self themes as well. There are a total of nine not-self themes of the centers in Human Design, although it gets much more complex than that as there can actually be not-self themes for any of what are called *bridging gates.* In my case, because I am what's called *single definition* with three centers defined, I have six not-self themes according to the system.

These not-self themes are ostensibly ways that the mind can interfere with the healthy or "correct" mechanics of the form. As a Sacral Generator, I am here to wait to respond, to never initiate, and to trust guttural "uh-huh, uh-uh" sounds, according to conventional Human Design wisdom. It's a little more complex than that, as the understanding of Generators was developed to also include cases where there are no sounds, although that is a point of much debate. Human Design purists will often argue that you can only trust a Generator's sounds, nothing else. I have heard that anything a Generator says is just a *mental story*. I find this belief abhorrent for many reasons I have gone into already, but I nevertheless found some value in experimenting with noticing the sounds I would spontaneously make. If I opened an email and sighed, I would note that sigh as perhaps an indicator that I don't really have energy to handle that. If I found myself spontaneously making "ooh" and "ahh" sounds, or if someone asked me a yes or no question and I had a confident, spontaneous "uh-huh," I took that as an indicator that I have energy for those things.

It is still an open question to me how much sacral sounds and sacral response work for Generators in the system versus how fundamental it is to all human experience. It is believed that Generators make these sounds more than other types, but in practice, I've never found that to be true. Some people seem to make a lot of sounds and others don't. There doesn't seem to be any connection to the bodygraph.

Either way, there's probably some validity in the idea that by noticing the sounds we spontaneously make, we can get clues into what we actually have energy for or not. Having a psychoanalytic background, I see this in terms of libido. If you are exploring Human Design and are a Projector, Manifestor, or Reflector, I would urge you to experiment with sacral response. It may be an indicator from the unconscious of what you have libido for or not. Everyone has libido and much of the work of psychoanalysis is learning where that libido is already invested, where it can be disinvested, and what it can be invested in.

In my first year of experimenting with sacral response, I would say it had a net positive effect of getting me to reflect on things I had committed to out of peer pressure, guilt, or expectations that others had of me, or that I had of myself. Noticing my sacral responses got me to be more honest with myself about those areas of life where I did not have the energy for something but had been lying to myself about it.

This is a similar effect to psychoanalysis, which is mainly about becoming aware of our unconscious desires. A big part of psychoanalysis is becoming aware of things we didn't know we wanted to do, as well as coming face to face with the ambivalence of desire. If I have one criticism of the idea of sacral response, it's that it does not honor this ambivalence. In psychoanalysis, we learn that we never fully want one thing or its opposite. There is always ambivalence that must be navigated.

In any case, in the beginning, I didn't experience any negative effects from experimenting with my strategy and authority. It would only be after years of practice that I found myself in a place where I had unconsciously internalized certain beliefs and habits so strongly that it was completely automatic to me and I was unable to operate in the world without reference to the Human Design System.

Even then, it was only when I stopped believing in Human Design that I actually noticed these effects. While I was deeply in it, I was pretty much unaware of any negative effects. Once I left, I became aware of some of the negative effects like forgetting my normal self and shutting down critical thinking skills. I realized that I had been in analysis paralysis where I was in a state of stress constantly analyzing my decisions. It was as if all my critical faculties were replaced with scrutiny using the Human Design System. When I had my break with the system, I suddenly began to rediscover my actual critical faculties. But again, these negative effects only emerged after years in the system. In the beginning, it helped me a lot. It was great for me to reflect on things I had committed my energy to that perhaps were no longer serving me.

The other part of my early Human Design experience was the not-self themes. This also felt healthy to me at the time, although in hindsight there are aspects of these beliefs which I now wonder about. I am no longer sure that it was beneficial to believe some of the things I came to believe about myself. The not-self themes are probably helpful to contemplate as they are part of the shadow, as Jung called it, of being human. It is only dangerous if we take on limiting beliefs about ourselves as a result of these contemplations.

In that first year of study, I learned a lot about my Undefined Ego which was ostensibly always trying to prove, and it actually did get me to stop engaging in pointless arguments. I achieved a sort of mindfulness. In some ways Human Design is not that different from mindfulness, which is funny when Human Design claims to be a system of getting out of the mind. But it operates a little similarly to, for instance, Cognitive Behavioral Therapy techniques.

By learning about the Undefined Ego I would find myself embroiled in online flame wars only to have a wake-up moment where I suddenly became mindful of what I was doing—mindful of the feeling in my body of being amped up emotionally and angry—and I was able to stop the cycle from continuing. Instead of automatically reacting I had a little wedge or gap that I was able to open up to suspend my habitual reaction.

In the work of French philosopher Henri Bergson he calls this gap the "zone of indetermination" and claims it is a feature unique to the more highly developed mammals like humans. A dog or a cat has a very small zone of indetermination. They respond by habitual reaction and if you instruct them to go against their habit (for instance not eating the treat) they can only hold out for a short time. Humans are able to hold out much longer.

In my case learning about my Undefined Ego gave me access to a gap where I was able to suspend my habitual reactions of fighting and arguing and to snap out of it a bit and get a safe distance. In this sense it was similar to mindfulness. Learning about the other not-self themes gave me similar insights. I do think there can be a positive effect to this type of reflection insofar as it can help to stop and notice when we are stuck in a habitual reaction.

The difference between my beliefs now and then is that now I don't see having a Defined or Undefined Ego as a real thing. I think the techniques I practiced are useful for anyone, regardless of their bodygraph. I also now see a danger which is that these techniques can be very helpful at one stage of psychological development (as they were for me at that point in my life), but I can see the other side as well, which is the limiting belief that people with an Undefined Ego should never try to prove anything.

As a side note, a few years before my break from Human Design I returned to one of my first loves: Jungian typology, particularly the Objective Personality System developed by Dave Powers and Shannon Renee. It is a deep, complex and insightful system for understanding personality. In my studies of that system I determined what personality type Ra is and I found that so much of what he advised met specific biases in his personality.

One of the aspects of his personality is that Ra takes responsibility to develop models and to gather patterns but he does not take responsibility to prove them in reality. It seems to me that he probably got a lot of criticism early in his development of Human Design demanding proof. In looking at people's bodygraphs he likely found that many of them had an Undefined Ego and it's a little bit convenient that he could then label those people as not-self for demanding proof. In Ra's formulation, it is only the not-self of those who have an Undefined Ego that demands proof. Their true self doesn't care if something is proven or not. That's a little too convenient, if you ask me.

For many years any time I would look into trying to prove aspects of the Human Design System I would remind myself that I have an Undefined Ego and I'm not here to prove. Even when I began seriously looking for proof (which we will go into in Chapter 14) I was told by many in the Human Design community that it was my not-self operating.

Learning about the other undefined centers also had some benefits but ultimately led me overall to what I would consider limiting beliefs.

With the Undefined Solar Plexus it was interesting for me to learn that I am not an emotional person according to the Human Design System and that my emotionality is said to be amplifications and even distortions of emotions that are outside of me. I mentioned this in the chapter on emotional control. When talking about my emotional life I described and rationalized my reluctance to fully go into emotional states as having deconditioned from being more emotional. Now I realize some of that could have been the power of suggestion by being told that my not-self is emotionally expressive and my true self is neutral. I may have unconsciously identified with a more neutral way of being and tried to achieve that ideal.

I can't know for certain but it seems to me that some of my emotional neutrality was learned and the way I learned it was by being told that my true self is "wired cold," as Ra puts it. I would monitor myself for emotionality and use emotion stopping techniques to regain my neutrality. I don't want to say this is entirely negative because in some ways this is like mindfulness and if I'm caught in a negative emotional space this might actually be beneficial for me to gain some perspective. As mentioned before, in CBT it is common to reframe emotions by saying "I am having the thought that I am feeling sad" rather than simply making the personal statement "I am feeling sad." That is an emotion stopping technique. It gives a safe distance.

I suppose the difference is that in Cognitive Behavioral Therapy, once you have that safe distance you can begin to explore the emotions again, whereas in my practice in Human Design I would simply get a distance from the emotions not to return to them because they ostensibly weren't my emotions to begin with. That is a sort of disowning of emotions that I think can be unhealthy.

For my Undefined Head and Ajna I was told that I have a tendency in the not-self to think about things that don't matter, and to pretend to be certain. For years I practiced thought stopping techniques without realizing that's what I was doing. I would use thought terminating clichés any time critical thinking would start. This was absolutely a limiting belief for me. Realizing that it's okay for me to think about anything and that there is really no difference between defined and undefined centers was frankly mind blowing to me. I was so sure for years of my life that the centers were real, the bodygraph was real, all of it was real. Only after much investigation and critical thinking on my own part have I come to the conclusion that Human Design operates through ambiguity, synchronicity and cognitive biases.

That still doesn't mean it's as simple as saying we should throw the whole thing away, although I'm also not precious about that.

Now again, these are all tools. There are people who are really neurotic and have racing thoughts all the time and learning a thought terminating cliché, a meditation technique, or something that reminds them to stop spinning out in their head could actually be hugely beneficial for their quality of life. I didn't have that problem so in my case it did more harm than good. And, ultimately, I don't think there's a real difference between having a defined or undefined center.

As mentioned, one of the negative aspects of the not-self I learned has to do with the Undefined Throat. From the very beginning I had a problem with this idea. I was told that people who have an Undefined Throat talk too much and should be silent more often. This really bothered me but I took my own adverse reaction to this idea as evidence of how deep the not-self was in me.

It's very much a catch-22 where if you're told something like this and accept it at face value then it becomes true, but if you reject it, your very rejection becomes evidence that it's true. There is no situation where it can be seen as false.

I rejected the idea of the not-self and began developing my own theories about it, but time and again throughout the 10 years that I was deeply in the Human Design System I would meet up against the same prejudices. At one point, I went to visit a well known Human Design figurehead in Europe. My experience was mixed. He was generous, funny, charismatic and genuinely caring.

And yet, he seemed determined to put me in my place—to make me realize that I was not living my design, that I was not-self.

On our first night meeting he told me I had to start over from scratch because I hadn't learned the first thing about deconditioning—that I ought to go back to the drawing board and start over at the beginning. He called me a "little child" and said that I had only become mentally fascinated with Human Design but had never taken the first step toward living my design. He said that, because I was so fully in my not-self, my Undefined Throat was "sucking up all the attention in the room." He said he had never met someone so fully in the not-self, that it was astounding how much I operated from my Undefined Throat's not-self theme.

At that point I had arrived with a friend who also had an Undefined Throat and he had another friend present who had an Undefined Throat, too. He indicated that his friend with an Undefined Throat, who remained silent while we spoke, was really living his design. In my case, my excessive talking, in his view, made it clear that I was not actually living my design. My friend who I brought along was a different story. He talked to her extensively, probably in no small part due to the fact that she is an attractive woman. She also had an Undefined Throat and yet he never once criticized her, even though they were talking at length for hours.

I had another friend I knew with an Undefined Throat who had always been quiet. She wasn't in Human Design so she hadn't learned anything about this. When I would bring it up to people they would just say that maybe she was naturally living her design more. And yet in her case she actually ran into a lot of trouble around wishing that she spoke up more. I believe it would have been perfectly healthy for her to learn to speak up more, to make her voice heard, to practice public speaking and projecting her voice. And yet, I can imagine most people versed in Human Design would say that she had made up a mental story around needing to speak up. You can see the problem here: I am perfectly happy being myself, speaking up for myself, and yet I am called not-self. She actually runs into real problems feeling she lacks a voice and would be encouraged to continue being silent and "get over" her mental chatter around not being heard—even though she really does run into problems from not being heard. She could actually improve her life by taking public speaking classes or working through some of her social anxieties around communication, but she would be encouraged to stay exactly as she is—to "practice self-love" which is often code for not trying to change in any way, while I would be encouraged to "start over from the beginning" because of exhibiting the supposed not-self theme of my Undefined Throat. It's ridiculous.

These not-self themes might give fuel for reflection but for the most part, they consist of authoritarian statements. The not-self theme of the Undefined Throat is always looking for attention. In other words, if you have an Undefined Throat, shut up. I think this is one of the most damaging things that Human Design readers tell their clients. Thankfully most Human Design readers don't go to that extreme. Most of them simply say it's about becoming aware of when to speak, when not to speak, and noticing who's paying attention or not. That is great advice for anyone. We should all be aware of when we are annoying someone by talking too much, when they're paying attention to us or when their attention is elsewhere. That's just good advice, but it has nothing to do with the bodygraph.

I also have an Undefined Spleen. The *not-self strategy* of the Undefined Spleen is holding on to things that aren't good for you. It was good advice for me to ask myself: am I still holding on to things that no longer serve me? Am I holding on to grudges? Am I keeping objects I don't use? These questions are probably healthy for anyone to ask themselves. I don't think there was much negative in being told that I should question whether things are healthy for me or not.

There is perhaps a slight negative effect of Ra describing the Undefined Spleen as "clingy" in relationships, somewhat akin to the anxious attachment style. This belief did not affect me too much as I just took it as a stereotype that should be overcome rather than a fact. But over the years I definitely came up against the assumption that I would be clingy because I have an Undefined Spleen. These kinds of negative stereotypes are rampant within Human Design communities.

If I had to summarize the benefits from my first year in Human Design they were:

Getting me to think about what decisions I had made where I had committed my energy;

Increasing my mindfulness of interpersonal dynamics through observing the not-self themes; and,

Getting me to ponder philosophically what my role is in the totality through profile and how people interact with each other.

It certainly expanded my horizons, gave me a lot to think about, and gave me new perspectives on the world.

Where it became limiting is the belief that aspects of my chart applied only to me and aspects of other people's charts that I didn't possess applied to them. I now believe that all aspects apply more or less to everyone and that the differences in how much a description applies to someone are based on a number of factors, none of which are the bodygraph except through synchronistic effects.

After that first year I got deeper and deeper into Human Design, eventually learning about what is called substructure: *color, tone,* and even going all the way to *base theory,* which is a highly complex and deep aspect of the Human Design System. I learned about *rave cosmology*. I learned *magic square* and *incarnation sequencing*. In each case it's a similar sort of effect where I greatly enjoyed pondering new and interesting areas of thought, while also picking up some limiting and often strange beliefs along the way.

I had the belief that if you aren't in the right *environment* you wouldn't be healthy or fulfill your purpose, so I had a very hard time accepting that my mother, who has *shores* as her environment and happened to live in a shore environment, could be healthy moving to the mountains where I live in Santa Fe, New Mexico. It turns out she is healthy here. Without realizing it, I had taken on indoctrinated phobias, irrational fears that actually had no basis in reality.

Similarly I began to eat strictly according to my dietary regimen (what's called determination or PHS, short for Primary Health System) because of the irrational fear that if I didn't follow a particular protocol I would not be healthy. I began monitoring how I see others and what I see in them—aspects of *view* or *perspective* and *motivation*. These are deeper areas of Human Design than many will go, but they yield even more mechanisms for control. They gave me all sorts of patterns o monitor in myself in order to control my own behavior. They also gave new ways of viewing reality which could, potentially, be expansive, or can be ways of controlling the narrative. Any time something happened, no matter what it was, I had dozens of concepts at my disposal that I could weave together into a story to suit my needs. If I had to make myself look good and make others look bad, or portray myself as in the right in a situation, I had countless ways of doing that.

I do appreciate the incredible smorgasbord of ideas, keynotes, and archetypal themes that Human Design gave me. It was like a playground for me, probably in part because of my personality and my own idiosyncratic interests. I am someone who loves playing with patterns and Human Design gave me what I felt at the time to be an inexhaustible wellspring of patterns to explore. Now I have a different view, but I am still thankful for those patterns, while I regret that I took them so seriously for such a long time.

CHAPTER 9: COMPARISON TO OTHER
SYSTEMS AND MOVEMENTS

IN THIS CHAPTER, I would like to compare the Human Design System and Human Design communities to other systems, organizations, and movements. I will be comparing Human Design to movements that have been called cults as well as new religious movements.

In some cases, there are clearly defined cults. For instance, Jim Jones's Peoples Church, the David Koresh group, and NXIVM (pronounced Nexium) are pretty much universally agreed to be cults. In other cases, like the Hare Krishna Movement (The International Society for Krishna Consciousness, ISKCON), or arguably Scientology or Landmark Forum, they are probably better described as movements. I am not in a position to state unequivocally that they are cults. I certainly personally feel that some of these movements meet the criteria for being cults in the various models we have explored here. But at least in the case of

Scientology, they have actually sought legal action against people who have declared that they are a cult in the past. This, to me, seems even more culty as it follows the criteria of information control. But again, I'm not saying Scientology is a cult, not least of which because I don't want to be sued by them. Use your own judgment here as elsewhere.

There was a period of time when I felt that Human Design was somehow primary, that Ra had access to what we call in Human Design source knowledge, and that any connections between Human Design and other systems were due to the fact that this source knowledge is somehow a universal archetypal truth that various other systems have touched on or sprang forth from. I essentially believed that any comparisons between Human Design and other systems were due to the fact that they both accessed the same source knowledge. Human Design presents itself as, to quote Ra, "an absolute of the maya," which is taken to mean that it has some fundamental priority over all models of reality.

I no longer believe that. Now I think it is just as likely that Ra was exposed to some of these other systems and drew influence from them.

I have tried to find out what kinds of books were on Ra's bookshelves. I have heard from those who knew him that he was a big fan of Theosophy, Helena Blavatsky, and Éliphas Lévi's work on ritual magic. He himself claims to have been studying Theosophy at the time that he had his prophetic encounter with the Voice. In Ra's *Encounter with the Voice* film, Ra claims to have been taken to Shambhala during his encounter. Shambhala, also known as Shangri-La, is the mythical abode of Sanat Kumara and the Ascended Masters in Theosophical tradition, as well as various Ascended Master traditions, like the I Am Movement and Elizabeth Clare Prophet's Lighthouse Movement. From this and other aspects of the system it seems clear that the Theosophical tradition was influential to Ra.

Incidentally, prominent reincarnation researcher Walter Semkiw on his website Reincarnation Research claims that Ra is none other than the reincarnation of William Quan Judge, one of three main founders of the Theosophical Society. For those who are more esoterically inclined, you may want to follow up on these mystical connections.

I am more interested in the influences Ra took from other systems, as well as potentially coincidental similarities between Human Design and other systems.

SCIENTOLOGY

A brief comparison of the Human Design System and Scientology follows. In Human Design, we have the not-self. In Scientology, it is called the "reactive mind." In both cases, this refers to the conditioned part of a person that acts based on societal pressure or trauma. Both are transcended through following a structured system.

In Human Design, we talk about deconditioning. That takes a minimum of seven years. In Scientology, this is called "clearing" or "auditing." It is the process of removing not-self or reactive influences. In Scientology, this is becoming "clear." They are lifelong, multi-step processes with layers and layers of deconditioning or clearing.

Human Design has strategy and authority. In Scientology, we find "tech" or "the bridge." These are prescribed methods to bypass conditioning. The tech is seen as the only reliable path to becoming clear. The conditioning field is the enemy—a homogenized world that keeps us locked in our not-self. In Scientology, this is the suppressive influence, suppressive people, and subconscious trauma imprints that they call "engrams."

In Scientology, your goal is to become clear, which is also called "thetan" or "operating thetan" (OT). Operating thetan is seen as the pure self, unclouded by conditioning or trauma, that can only be achieved through extensive effort. In both systems, the real you is seen as something hidden beneath layers of false identity.

Both Human Design and Scientology say that you can't trust the rational mind to make decisions. In Scientology, the reactive mind is the enemy.

Human Design gives you a set of traits based on your birth time. In Scientology, these traits are revealed through tests, like the Oxford Capacity Analysis. In both cases, heavy jargon and an air of scientific legitimacy aims to convince you that there's really a lot going on. And, to be fair, there probably is a lot going on. Humans are multifaceted people, and any sufficiently complex system will touch on aspects of that complexity.

Human Design also aims to give you some sense of your role in life through concepts like incarnation cross and profile. In Scientology, this is the *tone scale* that ranks emotional states, what are called *ethics conditions* and a ranking of behavioral states. Both Human Design and Scientology give you stages of ascension, something they share with Theosophical schools of thought.

Now, I don't want to say that all hierarchical models are bad. Erik Erikson's stages of maturational development, the stages of the evolution of consciousness in Spiral Dynamics, and the afore-mentioned Theosophical levels of ascension probably have some value. I am especially partial to the notion of ascension from Theosophical schools of thought because that is basically saying our life does have a purpose, and its purpose is the soul's evolution. Such spiritualist or mystical approaches don't really seem that problematic to me, although, of course, it depends what you do with them. But it is interesting to me how similar Human Design is to other systems and what explanations we might have for that. Again, I previously explained this as saying that Ra had special access to source knowledge and that other, similar systems were bastardizations or lesser copies of this fundamental knowledge. Now I am not so sure.

Continuing with our comparison to Scientology, in Scientology, you have auditors, also called case supervisors. They are trained intermediaries that interpret your psyche and your development. You can't figure it out on your own. You need the system and trained guides. Entry-level training encourages further investment on a path with a formal hierarchy of training and status levels. This is a gated path that can be climbed only through sanctioned education.

In Scientology, it is called "the bridge to total freedom," whereas in the Human Design System, it is a series of educational courses that give you legitimacy in the system. As someone who has never taken the courses myself, it came as no surprise to me that when I was seeking to teach Human Design, I was met with restrictions at official levels, informing me that I must achieve certification if I am to ever be taken seriously in the world of Human Design.

Even as late as 2025, when I had already decided to leave Human Design, I heard from someone who spoke with Lynda Bunnell, the head of IHDS. She was familiar with my work and impressed with what I had done with my conference, but urged our mutual friend to encourage me to go through the official certification process, a process requiring years of study and over $20,000 of investment. Perhaps she genuinely felt it would help me, or perhaps it was a way of maintaining control. I will never know because by that time I was already finished with my time in Human Design.

Looking at the founder dynamics and where authority is derived in Scientology compared to Human Design, we have Ra and L. Ron Hubbard who both claimed exclusive revelations. Ra claimed he got the entire system from a disembodied voice over eight days in 1987. Hubbard claims to have discovered it through research and spiritual insight. In Scientology, Hubbard's research is treated as infallible.

In both cases, they have an extremely precise system, perhaps because the level of detail and precision, as well as the specific use of language gives people the impression of expertise and mastery. In Scientology, the correct application of tech is sacred. This high level of precision is one of the areas in Human Design that made it very difficult for me to imagine it could be inaccurate. For one thing, there are some bullseye hits in any Human Design reading. I now believe this is because of the level of complexity and that any sufficiently complex system will have a few bullseyes. For another thing, the fact people could spend decades mastering the system made it seem impossible to me that the whole thing could be inaccurate or only operant through synchronistic effects. If it was presented as a mere set of beliefs, those beliefs could be challenged. The fact Human Design and Scientology are presented with an excessive level of complexity makes it hard to challenge them without first gaining expertise in the system, and even then, there is never really a point where you are enough of an expert to raise criticisms. In both systems the originators are the ultimate experts and have the final say.

In both cases, there is strict pressure to comply. In Human Design, this is compliance with your Type, Strategy, and Authority. In Scientology, it is called "ethics conditions." "You're not living your design" becomes "you're out of ethics" or "PTS" (Potential Trouble Source) in Scientology terminology.

Finally, they both share similarities at the level of cosmology and understanding of the evolution of humanity. For Human Design, this is about the *mutation* from the seven-centered to the nine-centered being. In Scientology, this is expanding to higher states or OT levels and the differentiation between pre- and post-OT.

Human Design has a rather science fiction idea of the *2027 mutation* and coming so-called *rave children*. In Scientology, this is the galactic role—a future where advanced beings regain interstellar power through advanced OT abilities.

I will continue this chapter by surveying some of the other systems that I became aware of in my investigations. I will leave it to the reader to draw comparisons to Human Design, and I will also give a warning. The following paragraphs are extremely jargon-heavy, bordering on word salad at times. Yet, I will try to be as accurate as possible using the terminology of each system. I will also rely on the reader to decide for themselves which of the systems and movements described in this chapter qualify as cults. Again, I am not calling any of these systems cults. I am relying on the reader to make up their own mind.

SPIRAL DYNAMICS AND INTEGRAL THEORY

I already mentioned Spiral Dynamics and Ken Wilber's Integral Theory. While I don't think it's quite as bad in some of the control departments, I have certainly been exasperated when talking to deep practitioners of this system who categorized every question or aspect of critical thinking into a system. There are thought-terminating clichés and ways of weaponizing Spiral Dynamics and Integral Theory to shut down actual critical inquiry.

In Integral Theory, you have quadrant roles and typologies, as well as an integral life practice, which is guiding principles for growth. You have development lines for specific faculties, as well as states and levels, aspects of consciousness. Finally, you have a personality spectrum that aims to describe you. Everything is put into hierarchical levels of consciousness and levels of evolution. The highest level, or meme as it is called, is unity consciousness.

This level is given the color teal or turquoise. Integral theory practitioners usually believe they are somewhere between that level
and the one below it, yellow, which is systematizing intellectual
thought. Ken Wilber himself believed he was between those levels.
There's a bit of false humility here. They don't say they're at the
absolute top of the most evolved. They say they're somewhere
between the second most evolved and the most evolved.

LANDMARK FORUM

Looking at Landmark Forum, which I mentioned before, everything is "rackets" or "stories." You can accuse people of running
a racket and this has the effect of silencing dissent. The term
"breakthrough" is highly significant and loaded, as is the term
"transformation." These are supposedly processes of discovering
who you really are and realizing things about yourself. The terms
"distinctions" and "structures" are also loaded. Again, these are all
terms that are used in the system to mean very specific things.

THEOSOPHICAL SYSTEMS

You can see there is a range of connections between Human
Design and other systems, from the more mundane to the more
mystical. Going to the mystical side, we have Theosophy, which
we already explored in part. But I didn't really use much of its
terminology. In Theosophy, you have a higher self called a
"monad," as well as a "dharma," or soul purpose. Your chakras,
or etheric centers, give you an energetic anatomy. You can identify
with "mayas" and are limited by "karmas." And you go through
an initiation process following the ascended masters' teachings,
the transcendent source of revelation that is taken as gospel.

In Anthroposophy, an offshoot of Theosophy developed by
Rudolf Steiner, you have "supersensible bodies," the etheric and
the astral. You have the duality of the physical and spiritual self,
or your inner and outer being, reminiscent of the Personality and

Design sides of the Human Design bodygraph. You do inner development and soul work, a personal purification process, which leads you to your karma and destiny, your life mission. There's also the evolution of consciousness epochs, as we found in Integral Theory and Spiral Dynamics.

Access Consciousness

Another system is called Access Consciousness, where you have "bars," which are energy nodes that unlock freedom from limitations. You also have limiting beliefs, false identifications that restrict being. It's interesting because I talk a lot about limiting beliefs, but I don't mean the same thing as what they mean in Access Consciousness.

What you'll find when you get into some of these systems is that they reuse a lot of the language that is used outside of the system, but they load it up with new significance. Normally when you talk about deconditioning, you're actually talking about deprogramming from limiting beliefs. But in Human Design, deconditioning means something else. Similarly, in Access Consciousness, limiting beliefs means something like the not-self in Human Design.

Access Consciousness gives you navigational logic with questions like "what would create more?" The system gives you the energetic release processes of clearing, similar to Scientology. You get "awareness points," insight windows into the self. You can see the cross-cutting similarities across many of these systems here.

NXIVM

An organization that has pretty much unanimously been agreed to be a cult is called NXIVM (pronounced Nexium). It is pretty similar to Human Design, scary enough. It uses a lot of fancy, technocratic, techno-spiritual language.

141

NXIVM has the Rational Enquiry Protocol (REP) which is a system for behavior correction via what they call structural logic. It all sounds very technical and fancy. NXIVM has the concept of disintegration which is basically emotional reactivity from trauma. I don't feel comfortable with someone using the language of trauma unless they have a background in psychology or medicine. Things like the Somatic Experiencing framework are a little suspect to me, although I'm sure they have some value. I have more of a problem when Human Design teachers use the language of healing from trauma without having a clinical background. I have been accused of being in a so-called fawn response and not living my design by someone who presents himself very much in the healing profession and uses all of the language of growth and personal development. Was he really trying to help me overcome my supposed trauma? Or was he just trying to control the narrative? We should ask the same question about the claim in NXIVM which supposedly facilitates healing from past traumatic events.

NXIVM gives you what they call EM tools, which are maps of psychological barriers, and allow you to develop your mission statement, a core life trajectory or life purpose. The EM process, or SASH rankings, gives you what they call introspective tech, which allows you to reprogram yourself. You can see the excessive amount of specific jargon makes it seem like there is a lot there. When hearing about these concepts, I must admit that my curiosity is piqued. If I was not familiar with some of the nefarious aspects of NXIVM like the founder literally branding his name on people and using sexual coercion and blackmail, I would be interested in learning about it. The terminology all sounds very sophisticated and if I didn't know better, I would probably research it with the assumption there must be something there. I mention this only to point out that any sufficiently complex and developed system gives the appearance of having depth and potential validity. For many years I found Human Design extremely deep. Now I am wondering if some of that is just an effect of the terminology and concepts used. Maybe these concepts weren't so deep after all, and it's just a fact that any system that gives us a new vocabulary for exploring reality will necessarily facilitate some level of introspection.

NEURO-LINGUISTIC PROGRAMMING

Some of what we are exploring also has similarities to Neuro-Linguistic Programming (NLP), a system that may help people at times, but also seems to me to have the dangers and risks of cult abuse and cultic control.

I first found NLP when I was around 14 years old. I was fascinated by it. I still think there are some compelling communication techniques and useful concepts. NLP uses the idea of submodalities, ways of internally representing things (e.g. auditorily, visually, kinesthetically) and develops various techniques loosely based on Milton Erickson's hypnotherapy practices for successfully conveying information. A lot of it is about sales techniques, but it could be used equally for therapeutic purposes. One of the main techniques put forth is the Swish technique for overcoming phobias, which seems to have some validity.

I got a lot out of my time studying NLP. I just think it has a high level for potential abuse, especially in its original form. You can read about some of the controversies around one of its founders, Richard Bandler who according to a 1989 article in Mother Jones, bragged about the copious amounts of cocaine he used. He was a charismatic, compelling salesman who developed communication techniques for a living, including the use of hypnosis and the power of suggestion. Again, I enjoyed learning NLP and I probably still use some of its communication techniques to this day. We just need to look at these systems in context. While it may be possible to separate the system from its creator, it's still important to have the context of knowing a little about the person behind the system.

RAELISM

Getting back to the mystical, or a sort of mystical-pseudoscientific hybrid, we have the system of Raelism which has many parallels to Human Design. In Raelism, there's the Elohim genetic upgrade. This is somewhat like the mutation in 1781, a mystical idea that we've undergone changes and now have access to new intelligences. There's the idea of cell encoded memory and DNA based consciousness. Raelism preaches advanced teaching protocols and neuro-energetic pathways. The protocols are the source to find your true self via an encoded truth hidden in your DNA. The neuro-energetic pathways, as they are called, are described as channels of perception or channels of awareness, reminiscent of the concept of channels in Human Design. In Raelism, humans are described as Elohim clones, reminiscent of the rebranding of humans as raves in Human Design. (Originally, all humans were described as raves, although later, Ra began using this term to exclusively mean a new form of human that would appear following a series of mutations.) Finally, in Raelism, the body is described as the technology of spirit.

All of these fancy concepts attain some level of cultural cachet from the fact they weave together jargon from the sciences as well as giving an air of technological sophistication. These systems don't obviously put forth beliefs. They seem more like techniques than belief systems. Indeed, for many years I denied that there are any beliefs in Human Design at all. I saw it as a collection of concepts and tools for self exploration.

THE AETHERIUS SOCIETY

The Aetherius Society is another mystical fringe group. They also talk of centers, as we do in Human Design, although they call them psychic centers or inner energetic architecture, which hearkens back to the chakra system. In the Aetherius Society, you have what's called your Earth mission, your spiritual life purpose, which is part of human evolution in the cosmic plan that they call the interplanetary change cycle. You receive cosmic transmissions that help you follow a divine structure. Ultimately, you have what they call the spark of God or inner light, which is the core divine component of humans

OTHER SYSTEMS

There are many more systems that we could draw comparisons to, ranging from relatively innocuous fringe beliefs all the way to full-blown cults. Many of these concepts may actually have some truth in them. From the Jungian perspective, these are archetypes. Ideally, they should be taken symbolically, figuratively, or appreciated aesthetically, even, for the post-Jungians, like James Hillman. What all the Jungians and post-Jungians seem to agree about is that they should not be taken literally.

It's an interesting question of what these archetypal themes indicate. Do they indicate fundamental truths? Possibly. But we have to qualify what we mean by truth. If we're talking about logical truths, it doesn't seem that the archetypes have much to say about that. If we're talking about factual truths, about the status of things, then it also doesn't seem like those truths are really best grasped archetypally. Those are what we could call literal truths. But if we're talking about greater truths of the human condition, and the truths of the psyche, what we might call psychological truths—although even adding "logical" to the end doesn't do it justice—ultimately, if we're talking about truths of the soul, it seems to me the archetypes have a lot to say.

The danger from a Jungian perspective is when these archetypal truths are taken literally, or when the archetypal complexes possess someone, causing what Jung calls an inflation. The inflationary state is when someone is possessed by an idea, pattern, symbol, image, or structure. That archetypal content takes over their life.

There is a great quote from Dr. Robert Moore, author of "King, Warrior, Magician, Lover," made all the more poignant by his own tragic story. Dr. Robert Moore sadly ended his own life and that of his wife in tragic murder-suicide. What more extreme example of an archetypal possession is there than when someone acts completely out of their regular character and commits a heinous act? Nevertheless, and perhaps made all the more poignant by this fact, Robert Moore has a statement about the nature of archetypes, which I think is highly relevant to our examination of these archetypal themes. His quote follows:

"I need to inform you now about the difficulty and danger of the archetype ego axis. The first thing I need to communicate is the seductive aggressive quality of the archetypes. These things are not passive, they are aggressive. They want you, and they want all of you, each one wants all of you. They are impersonal and imperialistic, and not only that, they are good at it, because once you connect with that numinous energy coming off these things, the seductive power of it is enormous, and it has the ability to overwhelm the critical powers of the ego more than almost any modern type can understand. Jung understood this. Archetypes are radioactive, contagious, and possessive."

—Robert Moore, *Practicing the Presence of the Other Within: Developing the Ego-Archetypal Self Axis*

CHAPTER 10: HOW DOES HUMAN DESIGN

WORK?

HERE WE COME TO one of the most interesting topics that I found in my explorations of Human Design as a belief system, the topic of how and why it is compelling as a system. Indeed, this question extends beyond Human Design. Why do we believe things? Why do we find some beliefs compelling and others unconvincing? How come certain stories can captivate us to the point they become our preferred interpretive lens of reality?

We touched on this briefly in the last chapter, but it seems to me the question of how Human Design can be a convincing model of reality is best explained through an understanding of cognitive biases on the one hand, and through an understanding of synchronicity, meaningful coincidence, and archetypal resonance on the other. These two approaches are, in some ways, two sides of the same coin: the rationalist, eliminative materialist approach, which dismisses the convincing qualities of these systems as gullibility, naïveté, and the placebo effect; and, the approach which sees these systems of meaning-making as fundamental aspects of a non-local consciousness built into the very fabric of reality.

We will be exploring both perspectives in the coming chapters. I am just laying out the overview of what we might call a range of perspectives from, on the one hand, people pointing fingers at astrologers and Human Design practitioners, or even those two groups pointing fingers at each other for being gullible, naïve, easily tricked, or susceptible to magical thinking. And on the other side, a more reverent respect for mysticism and the mysteries of life and consciousness.

They are both important. The reverent attitude toward the mysteries is highly susceptible to inflations of grandiosity and delusional thinking. The rationalist, materialist view is also susceptible to its own form of inflation, its own grandiose claims to have exclusive access to real objective truth from a supposedly neutral God's eye view from above. Both sides claim objectivity and it's not my goal here to privilege one or the other nor to exhaustively look at these two worldviews. I am painting in broad strokes here.

First of all, what do I mean when I say Human Design works? I suppose there are many ways that it works. A more nefarious way could be that it works by brainwashing you. A more charitable approach would say that it works by improving your life in some way. Either way, how are we to measure such a claim?

Ultimately much of our measurement is through self-report, and yet it is that same self-report that is suspect. We know that people can get Stockholm Syndrome where they self-report a positive relationship to their abusers. We know that people can get brainwashed where they self-report how much something has helped them when it has actually harmed them. We know that otherwise normal people participated in the Jim Jones massacre — that is an obvious harmful impact. And, we know there are other harmful impacts that are not so obvious: isolation from families and loss of self-identity, to name two.

It seems that the first question is really: what do we mean when we say that Human Design works?

Perhaps this could be rephrased. Why do people get into Human Design? Why does it captivate them? What psychological mechanisms are at work making them excited to learn more about it or put it into practice? Are there psychological qualities of the people, as is often claimed, such as gullibility, naïveté, or not having a strong sense of self? Or, more positively, qualities of openness and intelligence?

I don't think we can put much weight on personal characteristics. Particularly in the negative version, I often hear that the only people who come to take on fanatical beliefs are those who already want to give their power away. The idea goes that if you have a strong sense of self and strong critical thinking skills, you are immune to influence from such extreme beliefs.

I think it is quite arrogant to assume that anyone is immune to influence. It really depends a lot on the conditions. You could take the person with the strongest psyche, strongest sense of identity, healthiest sense of boundaries and greatest critical thinking skills and put them in a situation that is the right mixture of stressors, and they would crack.

I don't think it's the right path to analyze the people involved in the systems or try to find what's wrong with them that would lead them to believe something so apparently crazy. I'm sure there are some psychological traits like in the Big Five system—the trait of openness—that have some correlation, but it's not my goal to find the traits. I am more interested in the mechanisms at work that make things like astrology and Human Design compelling.

You will notice that I am grouping both astrology and Human Design here. This is because I believe that they work similarly.

149

When I told a friend who is quite a famous astrologer—who has given keynote speeches at the world's largest astrology conferences and hosts his own astrology conference—that I was leaving Human Design, he said that was great because it's so culty. He then gave about 20 reasons why, in my astrological chart and the current transits, it is my time to leave. To me that is equally culty. It is exactly the same thing I have a problem with: using a belief system in a limiting way to explain away choices and to terminate thought. Astrologers use just as many thought-terminating clichés as Human Design practitioners.

While it isn't a competition for which system has more cultic beliefs, I'm including astrology here because I believe it has some of the same potential dangers and perhaps same underlying mechanisms at work.

The real question is: what is this mechanism and why do we find ourselves so moved by systems like Human Design and astrology? What in them speaks to us, makes us feel seen, makes us excited to learn more, and sometimes even gives us a whole new behavioral protocol and an entirely new identity?

In the following 3 chapters we will explore aspects of this question. In our first foray we will look at cognitive biases. Then we will move on to the notion of synchronicity or meaningful coincidence. Finally we will look at the archetypes in more detail and examine the notion that archetypal themes have a special captivating power over the human psyche.

CHAPTER 11: COGNITIVE BIASES

IN THIS CHAPTER, we will review a number of cognitive biases that all seem to have something to do with why we find systems like astrology and Human Design compelling.

I say "we" here, although the fact is many do not find these systems compelling and often, or at least sometimes, have their own self-congratulatory attitude of superiority. I don't think this attitude is warranted. Each and every one of us should remind ourselves to stay humble and realize that even with the greatest skepticism and critical thinking skills, these cognitive biases exist and permeate our lives.

Yes, some people may exhibit some cognitive biases more than others, but even someone who reads through these biases and scoffs derisively at those who fall for them probably has a lot of other biases they aren't aware of. I do think it is helpful to learn about these biases because while we are never fully free from them, we can certainly gain the vocabulary to discuss, recognize and name them.

But at the same time, just as I've been warning against the addiction to categorizing things and putting them in boxes—playing the game of moral superiority—it's only too easy to do the exact same thing with cognitive biases. It's really a hall of mirrors where, just as I'm complaining about astrologers and Human Design practitioners using categories to explain away everything, it's just as annoying when someone uses cognitive biases to explain away everything.

There is a difference between explaining and explaining away, and we should strive for the former.

The Barnum / Forer Effect

The Barnum / Forer Effect is the bias that people tend to accept vague, general statements as accurate to themselves personally. An example would be saying, "You are brave and also timid. You are outgoing and shy. You are impulsive and yet you are also measured." By saying opposite or overly vague statements, people tend to agree. Why yes, I am both brave and timid! It is commonly known as the Barnum Effect because of the idea that showman and circus founder P. T. Barnum was known for hoaxes. It is more officially referred to as the Forer Effect, named after Bertram R. Forer who performed a classic experiment in 1948 demonstrating this effect. It was only later called the Barnum Effect in reference to so-called Barnum statements, generalizations often used by fortune-tellers and astrologers that are so vague they could apply to anyone, yet are presented as descriptions of the recipient. In Forer's classic experiment, he gave the following statements to a class of psychology students and asked them each to rate how accurate they were. He claimed that the statements were catered specifically to them, but in actuality, they all received the same set of statements. They are:

You have a great need for other people to like and admire you.

You have a tendency to be critical of yourself.

You have a great deal of unused capacity which you have not turned to your advantage.

While you have some personality weaknesses, you are generally able to compensate for them.

Your sexual adjustment has presented problems for you.

Disciplined and self-controlled outside, you tend to be worrisome and insecure inside.

At times you have serious doubts as to whether you have made the right decision or done the right thing.

You prefer a certain amount of change and variety and become dissatisfied when hemmed in by restrictions and limitations.

You pride yourself as an independent thinker and do not accept others' statements without satisfactory proof.

You have found it unwise to be too frank in revealing yourself to others.

At times you are extroverted, affable, sociable, while at other times you are introverted, wary, reserved.

Some of your aspirations tend to be pretty unrealistic.

Security is one of your major goals in life.

Forer's statements

The Barnum Effect is often cited as one of the reasons why people believe astrology. I am actually not too convinced by this one. I think a more compelling explanation for why astrology and Human Design can be convincing is because some of the statements actually are extremely accurate. There can be really precise, highly specific details about a person's life that really jump out. Over my years studying Human Design, there have been dozens of times where I've been taken aback at something so highly

153

specific there's no way "it" could possibly know. I've had a sense of wonder and amazement—how could this system, which doesn't know me, possibly know these things about me? How could a reader versed in this system tell me things about myself that are so intensely personal and specific?

If I'm getting a reading from someone and they tell me that I've found it unwise to be too frank revealing myself to others, that I have some aspirations that tend to be pretty unrealistic, and that security is a major goal in my life, I would basically kick them out. I would not be impressed in the slightest. There is virtually no impact of these types of statements, and my experience in Human Design shows me that, actually, Human Design readings and information derived from my own independent chart analysis can be nothing short of mind blowing. There must be a better explanation than the Barnum Effect, and I think there is. We'll go into that when we look at archetypes and synchronicity, which is a lot more convincing to me for a mechanism behind how it all works.

In fact, when I've told astrologers that cognitive biases may influence their belief in astrology, they often jump to the Barnum Effect as a way of dismissing cognitive biases in general as an explanation for why astrology is convincing. If you talk to astrologers who actually take their work seriously, they would never fall for the kind of ambiguous, vague statements that Forer used in his experiment. Astrologers would instead use highly specific statements, specific combinations of archetypal qualities to derive meaning. Someone might have Saturn conjunct Venus in their chart and be known for founding a society for the preservation of historical architecture. I believe Jackie Onassis is one such example. Astrologers might tell you how the combination of Saturnine archetypal qualities, like heavy old buildings and preservation combine with Venus, the appreciation of aesthetics, to explain her passion for the preservation of historic buildings.

That's very specific. There's no Barnum Effect there. The Barnum Effect would say, Jackie Onassis appreciates beauty, but also appreciates ugliness. She wants to preserve buildings, but she also wants to tear them down, and the like.

Since the Barnum Effect is not a very convincing argument, it's all too easy to reject all cognitive biases because of this fact—which itself, funny enough, seems to be a cognitive bias. We should not assume that just because the Barnum Effect does not adequately explain the appeal of astrology and Human Design, no cognitive biases are involved. The Barnum Effect is also suppos-edly what's behind cold reading by psychics, and I think that's probably a little closer to the truth, as psychics can use overly vague statements like, "I'm getting the sense that it's your family," instead of mentioning what member of the family it is.

When it comes to Human Design, astrology, or any suffi-ciently complex system, for that matter, I don't think that the Barnum Effect has much to do with convincing people of its veracity, because we tend to be convinced by the extreme speci-ficity of the system, not by vague or general statements.

That being said, there is one sense that it may influence us, and that is in saying contradictory statements. An astrological chart is so complex that you might find dramatically opposed themes. The same is true for a Human Design bodygraph. If you're trying to figure out where someone falls on a trait-based spectrum, like in the Big Five personality traits, you can narrow down where they lie through various approaches such as self-report and indepen-dent assessment. You might ask, is this person highly open, or do they have low openness? Are they agreeable or disagreeable? Through self-report and independent assessment you can eventu-ally narrow down where on a spectrum someone lies.

The problem with systems like astrology and Human Design is that you cannot narrow down a specific position this way.

Through self-report and independent assessment, while you may encounter contradicting views (e.g. someone seeing themselves very differently than how others assess them), you can negotiate these differences to eventually reach a conclusive statement: this person is high openness, low agreeableness, etc.

There are so many nuances of the Human Design chart that you can easily find support for agreeableness and disagreeableness in a chart, for openness and being closed off, and for many such oppositions. I think this is just the effect of having so many things going on. If the Human Design chart could be reduced to making predictions in five areas, like the Big Five trait analysis, then we could easily validate it or invalidate it. We could see what it predicts and see if that prediction is true or not. Instead, the Human Design bodygraph is unfalsifiable because it predicts exactly opposite things. Here is someone who is open and not very open. They're social and they're antisocial. On top of this, in case it wasn't bad enough having so many contrary predictions simultaneously present in the chart, Ra was also famous for adding "or not" to things. This was his get-out-of-jail-free card. Ra could basically say everything's a binary so it will either apply to someone or it won't. This made his system even more unfalsifiable and does admittedly result in the Barnum Effect. You can find extremely precise statements in a chart, but you can also find the opposite, so in that sense, the Barnum Effect probably is one of the reasons why Human Design is so convincing.

Confirmation Bias

Confirmation bias, also called cherry-picking of data, is another frequently cited cognitive bias that ostensibly explains why people believe things like astrology and Human Design. It is the tendency to search for, interpret, and remember information that confirms pre-existing beliefs. Believers in astrology often remember accurate horoscopes. They stand out.

It's sort of like being in a jazz band playing for the dinner crowd in a hotel lobby. Nobody notices you unless the whole band gets off and makes a big mistake. They only really hear it when it's clashing. In jazz you can kind of get away with it. A better example might be some highly consonant classical music where accidental dissonance stands out.

We don't really notice the vast majority of what's going on. We aren't scrutinizing every statement made, every keynote in the bodygraph. If you get a Human Design reading and count all of the statements made about yourself, it probably numbers in the hundreds. If we remember five or ten of those statements that really hit, we essentially select or cherry-pick the ones that stand out, ignoring the rest. This is confirmation bias at work.

We are scanning the noise for signal. If we get 200 statements out of a reading, most of them pass by as noise, but the handful that stand out as signal can go a long way in convincing us of the reality of the system. We might be astonished—how the hell did they know that specific detail about us?

Randy Richmond talked about how he gave a reading to a man who had Gate 59 Line 4, one of the 384 possible line placements in the bodygraph. He told this man that he needed friendship first before any possibility of sexual bonding. This is because Gate 59 is in the Channel of Intimacy and Line 4 is about friendship. This man was astounded. How the hell did this guy know that?

Well, there may be a bit of Barnum Effect as well as confirmation bias here. It sounds really specific, but if you get down to it, it's actually not that specific. It's not as specific as saying your wife is named Jane and your son is named Bobby and you work as an airline pilot and you once climbed Mount Everest. It's not actually that specific at all. It's simply saying you need friendship before you can be sexually intimate, which is something that I imagine a lot of people would agree with.

But even if that is something that really struck this man as highly specific to his life, there's the confirmation bias that he may have picked that one statement out of dozens of statements that basically passed by without standing out.

This one very much ties in to how Human Design works because it has to do directly with beliefs. We cherry-pick based on pre-existing beliefs—in other words, we believe something ahead of time, and then find the data that matches those beliefs, ignoring the rest of the data that doesn't fit our picture of reality.

It's pretty hard to get people to see confirmation bias, particularly if they don't think they believe in Human Design in the first place. I've literally told people in Human Design about confirmation of pre-existing beliefs only to be met with the claim that Human Design is not a belief system and that they actually don't believe what I imagine they do. While that may be true—I'm not an authority on what other people believe—I must also point out the fact that it is possible to believe something without being aware that we believe it. This bears repeating. We can wholeheartedly believe something and have zero awareness that we believe it. That, itself, should give us pause.

Of course, making matters worse, there will be a lot of people out there who don't believe this fact. They believe that they are aware of their beliefs. They believe that they know everything they believe, and if they say they don't believe something, they damn well don't believe it. This is what we could call a pre-analytic or pre-critical stance. This is a sort of naïve optimism that we actually know what we believe, or, put another way, that we know everything we know. Psychoanalysis shows us that there are lots of things we "know" (i.e. believe) that we are not actually aware of knowing or believing.

As I've said many times in this book, I don't want to make any assumptions about what others believe. For all I know, they could be right when they say they don't believe in Human Design. But from my perspective, it sure seems like there are a lot of strong beliefs going around, even the belief that Human Design is not a belief system.

SELF-SERVING BIAS

The self-serving bias (described originally as self-serving biases, plural) is a concept that came out of multiple studies in the 1970s in the field of psychology, including social psychology research by Miller and Ross. The self-serving bias occurs when a person attributes positive outcomes to oneself and negative outcomes to external forces. It's like the classic Hodja joke where Hodja is in an archery competition and keeps missing, and each time he explains that he is demonstrating how not to shoot the arrow, going through the various other contenders explaining that he is showing how they do it, until he finally hits a bullseye: "And that is how Hodja does it." When things don't go the way we want or expect, it's all too easy to cast them off on others. When, by some chance occurrence, things go right, we quickly identify with being the reason for that.

This relates to Human Design on two levels. The personal level, where an individual identifies positive outcomes in their life because of things they did, like following certain tenets of the system "I waited to respond and something good happened for me." And, on another level, ascribing positive outcomes to learning the system itself.—"Human Design works because I've experienced positive outcomes since I learned the system." The belief is that awareness of the underlying mechanics of the maya as they are referred to in Human Design itself has some effect that leads to positive outcomes in one's life, no action required.

There is a tendency to ignore or externalize negative outcomes such that when something bad happens, it can be easily dismissed as the not-self and not following design. Personally, I have done this many times. As a Generator, I ascribed positive outcomes to waiting to respond, and when negative outcomes happened, I would basically say, "Well I guess I initiated," or, "I guess my mind interfered. I'll have to do better next time."

THE ILLUSORY CORRELATION

The illusory correlation is a cognitive bias identified by husband and wife team Loren and Jean Chapman in 1967. This can be described as perceiving a relationship between variables without statistical evidence. We may have anecdotal evidence, which can be confirmation bias, but there's not actually any statistical evidence to support that. In other words, the plural of anecdote is not data.

This one is hard for me because I naturally, probably like a lot of people, think that once I've seen something over and over again, I have enough data. But the fact is, it's not actually statistically significant.

When I was learning about Manifestors, I began to guess who some famous Manifestors were and I was right. I guessed that Orson Welles was a Manifestor. I guessed certain friends of mine were Manifestors. I began to track other Manifestors and group them all together in the same bucket, and once I had 15 or 20 Manifestors, I started to look for patterns and commonalities.

Well, 15 people is not statistically relevant, and then the problem is now that I know hundreds of Manifestors, it's still not statistically relevant because I'm not able to really identify commonalities among them in a testable way. It would be testable if I started noticing that Manifestors usually have red hair and then I got a certain number of Manifestors and actually tested out my hypothesis—how many of them have naturally red hair? That's a testable hypothesis. But when I'm just considering a handful of people that I know, it's easy to fall into the illusory correlation. It's easy to think there's a correlation where there isn't one, simply because of a lack of sample size, let alone the lack of a testable hypothesis.

The Availability Heuristic

The availability heuristic, discovered in 1973 by Amos Tversky and Daniel Kahneman, overestimates the importance of information that comes easily to mind. The more memorable something is and the easier access we have to it, the more important we tend to think it is. Something we don't know much about that's hard to understand, complex, and not at the top of mind may just not seem all that important.

For years, I repeated slogans and thought-terminating clichés from the Human Design System to the point where they were always at top of mind. Anything that came along, I was able to say, *the most important thing is*—and immediately pick some simple, easy statement. *The important thing is to remember to wait to respond. The important thing is to wait for emotional clarity. The important thing is to remember to surrender to the form and not let the mind interfere*, and many other such truisms. There was always another cliché that came easily to mind, and because it came so easily, it seemed more important.

Selection Bias

Selection bias is another meaning of cherry-picking the data. You can get false positives or false negatives due to a non-random selection of data or experiences. A simple example: perhaps people who stay in Human Design for a long time have coincidentally received readings or coincidentally have bodygraphs that are highly accurate. I'm not saying this is the case because I tend to think the bodygraph is a bit more random than that, but let's just say for the sake of argument that 1 in 10 people gets a highly accurate bodygraph and the other 9 out of 10 get inaccurate ones.

Well, that 10% of people that get accurate bodygraphs may have a higher likelihood of getting into and staying in Human Design because of how accurate it is for them. Let's say you survey them and try to determine how accurate the bodygraph is. You'll get skewed results because you're not actually surveying a random population—you're surveying a selected population. This is selection bias at work.

This can also happen when we select from our own memories, only remembering what seems relevant, what seems accurate at the time, and forgetting all the times when it was less accurate.

Post Hoc Ergo Propter Hoc Fallacy

Now we're on to classical logic. The post hoc ergo propter hoc fallacy is a logical fallacy where we assume that because one thing follows another, it was caused by it. I tend to think that if my life improves after I begin experimenting with my strategy and authority, it is because I followed my strategy and authority. It could be, or it could not be. We should remember that just because something happens after something else, what follows is not necessarily caused by what precedes it.

If we find that it happens at scale or it happens over and over again, it gets more convincing that there's a causal relationship. The same is true if we discover the mechanism behind it. By understanding gravity, if I drop a glass and it shatters on the floor, I can pretty clearly say there is a causal relationship between me dropping the glass and it shattering, not only because it's a repeatable experiment but because we understand the mechanism behind it.

In the case of Human Design, we do not understand the mechanism behind it, and it is not a repeatable experiment. So in that case, it becomes much harder to say what the cause was. It could be that I was at a critical time in my life where I was reflecting a lot on how things were going and getting excited about self-improvement. Around that time, I discovered Human Design, and then my life got better. Who's to say that my life got better because of Human Design or because I was actually ready for self-improvement, or neither of those things—it simply got better on its own?

Besides, what do we really mean by "got better"? It's not really measurable. If we're trying to actually see what effect Human Design has, it would be better to try to formulate things in a more precise way. Unfortunately, so many of the improvements in one's life are hand-waved away using Human Design jargon: *I have greater satisfaction now, I meet less resistance, I am on the correct trajectory.*

TEXAS SHARPSHOOTER FALLACY

Let's look at the Texas sharpshooter fallacy. This is a bias where we ignore differences and focus on similarities. This is again related to the selection bias and the confirmation bias—it is basically cherry-picking. We notice similarities and we don't notice differences.

I might take a handful of Manifestors or Projectors and notice a few similarities within each group, taking that as validating that those divisions actually exist. But I might ignore the vast differences between members of each of those groups and the fact that those similarities might be explained better through another categorization scheme, or that those similarities may also exist between different groups.

THE ANCHORING BIAS

The anchoring bias is relying too heavily on the first piece of information encountered—the anchor. This was discovered by Tversky and Kahneman in 1974. This is also related to belief, so it is one that I'm very interested in. It's not a logical fallacy. It has more to do with our beliefs.

When we come to believe something, for instance getting a reading that seemed accurate, that first reading anchors us in our belief and can outlast a lot of subsequent irrelevant readings. An early accurate reading or an early belief can go a long way. We are anchored in it and can essentially withstand much of the randomness and lack of evidence that follows.

THE BELIEF BIAS

This is also similar to the belief bias explored by Evans, Barston, and Pollard in 1983. The belief bias states that we may judge the strength of arguments based on how plausible their conclusions are, rather than the strength of their arguments. We might accept flawed reasoning, or even an entire lack of reasoning or arguments, simply because we like the outcome or we already believe in what it is saying. It's basically a fancy way of saying that we can look past a lot of flawed reasoning if we like the outcome.

If Human Design ultimately says you are here to fulfill your life purpose and live a life full of happiness, we might like that idea so much that we look past a lot of things. Ra might make logical leaps or his reasoning may be full of logical fallacies, but we tend not to mind so much as long as we agree with the conclusion.

THE AUTHORITY BIAS

Next, the authority bias. This was famously explored by Stanley Milgram in his obedience experiments of 1961. We tend to value the opinion of an authority figure too highly. If a trusted friend, celebrity, teacher, or supposed expert promotes a system, we might give it more of a chance than we would otherwise.

This is something I personally had to work through in terms of my own guilt over promoting Human Design, ultimately coming to the conclusion that it's not so bad because it at least gets people thinking. But it is also partly why I feel an obligation to continue sharing my negative experiences with the Human Design System.

I feel like I owe it to the people who got into the system because they trusted me.

I am by no means a celebrity, but I do have some minor celebrity status in Human Design circles, and I certainly have gotten a number of friends into Human Design. I have felt personally responsible to share with each of those friends my negative experiences so they can come to their own conclusions.

While I don't see myself as an authority, even just the fact that I have a certain stature in the Human Design community gives me a level of authority that I have to acknowledge. And because I have that authority, I also have a responsibility to those who have trusted me.

The Hindsight Bias

The hindsight bias, discovered by Baruch Fischhoff in 1975, is the belief after something happens that it was explained or predicted ahead of time, even though the earlier prediction was quite vague. For instance, in astrology, the conjunction of Neptune and Uranus may be seen after the fact to have predicted the advent of the internet. I guarantee there were no astrologers back in the 70s and 80s who were making that prediction. True, the general prediction might loosely fit what actually happened. But if the internet hadn't been made at that time, we might just as easily find something else that loosely fits those predictions.

Pattern Recognition Bias

The pattern recognition bias is an interesting one. This is also called apophenia, a term coined by Klaus Conrad in 1958. It was originally named in the context of schizophrenia, but later broadened. This is the tendency to perceive meaningful patterns within random data—seeing faces in clouds or seeing patterns in any sort of random static.

This is a natural tendency that all of us have, but it is especially pronounced in schizophrenics. It is probably also more common in certain personality types than others, depending on how much someone is attuned to seeing patterns. Apophenia may explain why it is easier to find meaningful patterns when you have enough data. If Human Design only had a handful of data points it would be hard for a meaningful pattern to emerge. However, the body-graph has literally thousands of data points, making it much easier to weave a coherent story from the data.

THE NEED FOR COGNITIVE CLOSURE

The need for cognitive closure is an idea that was developed by Ari Kruglanski in 1996. This is a preference for firm answers and an aversion to ambiguity.

The preference for firm answers means that any system made up of statements delivered with conviction will simply be more convincing than one that comes across wishy-washy or overly ambiguous or vague. I remember one lecture where Ra claimed that to be a good reader, to give good Human Design readings, you have to deliver them with conviction. If you deliver the reading with skepticism or doubt—if you include the possibility it might or might not be accurate—it just doesn't land the same. A big part of Ra's guidance on how to give readings was to get people to deliver readings with what he called the right frequency. Well, that frequency, it seems to me, is confidence and conviction.

SURVIVORSHIP BIAS

The survivorship bias is focusing on successful cases and ignoring failures. We remember successful predictions and ignore the ones that didn't work out. We remember when something positive happens and forget all the negative things.

There is also survivorship bias at work in Human Design communities, where the people who stick around the community are those who have found some value in the system. If you ask people in the community what value they have found in following their strategy and authority, you're not getting a real sample size of all the people who have experimented with Human Design. You're getting the survivors of it.

SUBJECTIVE VALIDATION

Subjective validation is the tendency to perceive statements as true if they are personally meaningful, even if vague. This is closely related to the Barnum Effect. It was formally explored by Snyder, Shenkel, and Lowery in 1977.

If we experience something as relevant to us in a personal way, the very fact that it's talking about something deep and personal gives it credence. If it was making a rather impersonal prediction that didn't have much to do with us, we might hold it to greater scrutiny. But the moment it begins to talk about something deeply personal, it is easier to believe that it is accurate.

There have been a few times over the years that I questioned my own approach in readings because of touching on a personal, emotional topic, sometimes resulting in the person I was reading for having a strong emotional reaction. I told myself not to shy away from personal topics, and I do think there is value in exploring such areas, but I am also not a trained clinician, nor do I have any desire to be someone's therapist. I mostly did recorded readings for people in part because of this apprehension around broaching such deeply personal subjects. I also did my best to leave things open for people to draw their own conclusions.

I remember one case where I was talking about the Undefined Ego not-self theme, which can be formulated as feeling undeserving, or even questioning whether one has any value at all. The person I was giving a reading to burst into tears—I had struck a nerve. Overall, I think they had a positive outcome of exploring negative feelings and, hopefully, letting go of those feelings to come to find a greater sense of self-worth. We have to examine our negative feelings and beliefs in order to work through them, and I hope that I facilitated that process. That did give me pause, though. Was it the case that she truly had those feelings, or was the power of suggestion at work? Was I telling her that she felt a certain way because of her bodygraph? These questions led me to move away from in-person readings and to adjust my reading style. I saw how easy it would be to take these occurrences as confirmation that my readings were working, having an impact, and potentially lead me to self-aggrandizement. I saw that same self-aggrandizing tendency in other Human Design analysts and teachers, on their high horse feeling that they held the keys to unlock the truth in others. I was not comfortable being put in that position of power, and more so, I questioned whether exploring deeply personal issues ought to be reserved for therapeutic practice with trained professionals.

THE PLACEBO EFFECT

The placebo effect is a big one. Some people say that astrology only works through the placebo effect. I think that would be ignoring all of the other biases at play. It's also an interesting question of whether the placebo effect actually has more power than we might imagine.

The placebo effect is described as a belief in the effectiveness of something that causes psychological or physiological improvement. By its very definition, there is a real improvement that comes from that belief. This is an interesting one because it really is looking at the deep connection between beliefs and outcomes.

If we believe something will have a good outcome, it can sometimes actually affect that outcome. I say sometimes because obviously a gambler believing they're going to win the jackpot doesn't make it so. Nevertheless, someone taking sugar pills, believing they're getting real medicine, may still show improvements as if they were taking real medicine.

THE SUNK COST FALLACY

When I was reflecting on how difficult it was for me to extricate myself from my role as a figurehead in the Human Design community and how much my identity was wrapped up in it, I thought of the sunk cost fallacy. Also known as the escalation of commitment, this is when you continue a belief or investment due to previously invested resources.

Essentially, it means the longer you have believed in something, the more likely you are to keep doubling down rather than questioning it. When confronted with cognitive dissonance or a situation where you normally might reality test—that is, see if it actually is true in reality—instead, you put off reality testing because you've gone so long without reality testing in the first place.

I went through quite a head trip asking myself how I could change directions now, at this point in my life. Funny enough, and perhaps a positive point in favor of Human Design ideology, if we can call it that: I actually used a lot of the same language of empowerment I had used to justify my commitment to Human Design in my own rationale for leaving Human Design. That is, I actually reasoned that I was trusting myself, I was following my true life path, and any fears about what people would think or how I would make the shift away from Human Design were just conditioning from outside forces, i.e. peer pressure. I ended up pretty much using the language of Human Design to justify why I should leave Human Design, as an act of radical self-trust, and why I shouldn't be concerned about the sunk costs of having spent so long so deeply embedded within its worldview.

Still, I did have to go through a whole emotional process around it. I questioned whether I had wasted time, and what people would think of me for going against my previous highly public commitment. I wondered if people would trust me, or if they would be angry or disappointed with me. Indeed, in private conversations with friends, students and colleagues, I did encounter a range of emotional reactions, as I had expected. I accepted them with all the grace and equanimity I could muster, as I do now. I don't blame anyone for being disappointed with my change of heart. I continue to hold strong in my belief that there is no such thing as wasted time, a belief which carries me through this new direction my life has taken.

THE GAMBLER'S FALLACY

The gambler's fallacy is the belief that past random outcomes predict future random outcomes, when actually the random events have nothing to do with each other. If I flip a coin and get heads nine times in a row, I might be pretty sure that I will get heads on the 10th flip. But assuming the coin isn't weighted, there's actually no higher chance of getting heads than there was before.

It is a fallacy to think that all things being equal, random chance events influence each other. If they did, they wouldn't be random.

In Human Design, someone may make a series of accurate predictions in a reading, which then emboldens them to believe that they are likely to continue getting hits. That is, assuming that the bodygraph is random. Of course, one of the main conceits of Human Design is that it's not random. Or rather, the seeming randomness of being born at a particular time actually carries within it a highly significant ordered set of information that can be decoded.

But this is a conceit that has not been proven and may never be proven. I will explore this in the next chapter when we look at scientific attempts to validate Human Design and astrology.

THE BASE RATE FALLACY

The base rate fallacy, also called base rate neglect, is when we ignore statistical general information, base rates, in favor of anecdotal or specific cases. This is when we focus too much on anecdotes. We have plenty of specific examples where a prediction comes true. And yet, we aren't doing statistical analysis of a large enough sample size to determine whether that accurate prediction was merely the effect of pure chance.

If I devise a machine that I claim can always hit the bullseye in a game of darts, and I test it three times and get three bullseyes, I might think that I have proven it. But that's not true. I could test it a hundred more times and the next 97 attempts might not hit a bullseye.

It turns out there are well-founded studies in the field of probabilities and statistics that tell us just how many samples we need to get to a certain level of confidence. I actually had a friend years ago who worked at Amazon, a very smart guy. He would get hired freelance on the side to do experimental design. This means he was actually designing science experiments.

He would get hired by a science team who would bring him in to review their experiment. They would say, "We've tested for soil contamination and we have a sample size of 40,000 and we've tested for three different types." And he would say, "Actually, you have a sample size of three. You've just tested these 3 samples 40,000 times."

He would have to tell them that what they thought was their sample size actually wasn't a sample size at all. He would validate their experimental design. One thing I learned talking with him is that even incredibly smart teams of scientists would often design experiments in a way that did not hold up to scrutiny by mathematicians and experimental designers like him.

It was good enough to be convincing for the team in question and even good enough to get quite a bit of money from grants, but it didn't hold up to his level of scrutiny. The moral of the story is that even very smart people often make mistakes when it comes to designing science experiments. They often misunderstand what actually constitutes a sample size and how to design an experiment in a way that actually proves what they're trying to prove.

Quite frequently, they come to the conclusion that their experiment proves their hypothesis when it does no such thing. This is among scientists, so you can imagine how bad it is when people are simply using anecdotes like, "I know Jim, Billy and Sally and they're all Manifestors, and they're also jerks, therefore Manifestors are jerks." That kind of thing is just poor critical thinking.

MISATTRIBUTION OF AROUSAL

There's another interesting bias called misattribution of arousal. This has to do with mistaking the source of emotional responses. It was studied by Dutton and Aron in 1974. This is the discovery that emotional arousal has a sort of blanket effect where even a strong negative emotion like fear can be mistaken for attraction.

There's a classic joke where a behavioral psychologist is away on a trip with a colleague he's attracted to. He's learned that states of heightened emotional arousal can lead to, or be mistaken for attraction, so he decides to take her on a rickshaw ride. Sure enough, the rickshaw driver is weaving around corners and getting in near misses with other drivers. She's completely exhilarated by the experience. After they get off the rickshaw, he asks her what she thought. She tells him she's never had an experience like that. She tells him she hasn't felt so alive in years. And then she asks, does he think the rickshaw driver is single?

Sometimes we get a strong emotional response out of the person we're giving a Human Design reading to. If they feel understood or excited after a reading, they might attribute that feeling to the Human Design System or the person giving the reading, rather than other things going on in their life. Maybe they just went through a big breakup and they've been going through a lot emotionally. When they get a reading, something really clicks for them and they feel deeply understood and cared for. They might misattribute that feeling to the system, rather than to the many factors going on in their life at that time. Just the fact that readings can touch on some intense emotional triggers can lead to this effect. As mentioned before, I've had people burst into tears during readings. It's no surprise that, having gone through such a strong emotional experience, they might then come around having emotional attachments to the system.

THE EXPOSURE EFFECT

The exposure effect is also at play here: the more familiar we are with something, the more we tend to prefer, accept, and feel attached to it. Social psychologist Robert Zajonc proposed this bias in 1968, finding that repeated exposure makes things feel more credible.

The more you see memes and jokes about Human Design, or other people talking about it, or even simply day after day of reading about it or listening to lectures, it eventually begins to seem a lot more normal. In the beginning, you might hear some of the bizarre stuff claimed by Ra, like that there's a new energy type that emerged in 1781, we're evolving toward eventually becoming an immortal silicon-based lifeform called the Eron, we now have a new form of cognition called *rightness*, and we're mutating towards a new form called the rave. That might all seem quite bizarre, but the more you're exposed to it, the more normal it sounds.

The Clustering Illusion

The clustering illusion is the tendency to see patterns in small sets of random data. This is related to apophenia and the law of small numbers. This has to do again with sample size and neglecting the base rate. By getting a cluster of patterns in a small sample set, we naturally find it compelling, even though that pattern would go away if we expand the sample set larger.

The Attribution Error

The attribution error, also known as the fundamental attribution error, means we overvalue personality-based explanations rather than situational ones. We tend to naturally think things have to do with a certain person rather than other factors.

I mentioned this earlier when I said that one of the questions that comes up around cults is what kind of people get into them. We have a natural desire to attribute things to certain personality traits or character flaws. This is also victim shaming or victim blaming. It happens in court cases all the time where they get character witnesses to attest to an accuser having poor character. We tend to overvalue character or personality-based explanations, so one of the first things to do when defending Human Design against criticisms is to start calling the one making the criticisms not-self, not living their design, or not on the correct trajectory.

The Optimism Bias

The optimism bias is believing one is less likely to experience negative events than others. We tend to think bad things would never happen to us. We tend to be basically optimistic that we're more likely to experience positive things happening to us. Neil Weinstein studied this in 1980, finding that people tend to be unrealistically optimistic about life events.

How this applies to Human Design is that we may assume that we would never fall into cult-like beliefs, or be easily tricked. We may optimistically assume we have stronger critical thinking than we do, or that we aren't perpetuating some of the negative cultic qualities I'm talking about. Of course, I don't mean to imply that everyone who studies and practices Human Design is perpetuating negative cultic qualities. But if they were, most wouldn't realize it. Like my friend Von Paul says, why worry if you're crazy—if you are, you'd be the last one to know anyway. Still, contrary to his point, I do think it's worth examining our beliefs, as I hope all of us reading this book are doing now. I realize this in-depth examination of cognitive biases can be quite tedious, but I think it is a worthy effort and goes a long way in becoming aware of some of the pitfalls any of us are capable of falling into. Accepting that all of us are susceptible to these cognitive biases is an important step in becoming aware of them. If we are overly optimistic about our susceptibility, if we think it's impossible that we would ever fall into these cognitive traps, we certainly don't stand a chance of actually overcoming any of these biases.

PSEUDODIAGNOSTICITY

Pseudodiagnosticity is evaluating evidence without considering alternatives. It's basically looking at things without comparing. We may only use one explanation without trying on others. Doherty, Mynatt, Tweney, and Schiavo studied this in 1979.

This has been one of my hobby horses the last few years at the High Desert Human Design Conference. For a few years now I have offered alternative explanations for many of the traits described in Human Design. One of the other systems I've used is the Objective Personality System (OPS), as mentioned in Chapter 8, which offers a compelling alternative explanation for much of what is attributed to aspects of the bodygraph. It's not enough to say that Human Design explains ourselves and the world well. We have to actually try other systems of explanation to see if they have as much or more explanatory power. For years now, I have seen people attribute certain aspects of a person to gate, line, color, tone, channel, or any number of aspects of the bodygraph, which I feel are better explained by systems like OPS. Without going too in-depth into the system, I'll just list a few of the areas of overlap where OPS seems much more convincing in its ability to describe and predict aspects of a person's behavior and psychological makeup, with the added benefit of being independently verifiable. Human Design expects us to trust that what the bodygraph says is canon. OPS uses independent verification through assessment to determine characteristics, resulting in an arguably more scientific approach. (I say arguably because there are still some valid criticisms of OPS methodology, but it at least makes an attempt at independent verification through its use of numerous third party assessments.)

Here is a partial list of overlapping areas in OPS and Human Design (opposite page):

Human Design	OPS
Intuition is stronger for those with a Defined Spleen; inconsistent for Undefined Spleen.	Intuition is a form of perception; preference for using intuition can be verified by independent assessment.
Feeling is a continuous wave for those with a Defined Solar Plexus; those with Undefined Solar Plexus are "wired cold" and fundamentally emotionally neutral.	Feeling is a form of judgment; preference for being continually aware of one's emotions can be verified by independent assessment.
Logic is a circuit group and you can tell how logical someone is by their activations in this group.	Logic is a form of judgment; preference for logical reasoning can be verified by independent assessment.
Living your true self means not caring what other people think, overcoming a fear of being judged by others.	Some people (like Ra) are naturally unafraid of being judged. While it's good advice to overcome this fear, people of Ra's personality type naturally don't have much of a problem in this area, so it's a case of Ra telling other people to be more like him.
Living your true self means being in touch with what you want—"enlightened selfishness."	Some people (like Ra) are naturally more in touch with what they want, and out of touch with what others want. While we should all get in touch with what we want in life, people of Ra's personality type naturally don't have much of a problem here, so it's another case of Ra telling people to be more like him.

There are plenty more examples but most of it amounts to two things—first, that the bodygraph claims to tell you aspects of how you operate. And, second, that living your design consists of a set of qualities which "coincidentally" happen to be the same characteristics Ra has.

To the first point, the bodygraph is saying this person is wired to be intuitive while that person is wired to be emotional. OPS relies on independent assessment where you have a group of practitioners that review a recorded interview with the subject and come to their own conclusions, only later sharing notes on what they saw. They have a number of indicators to look for to determine if a person is intuitive, if they are a feeling type, if they have a preference for logical reasoning, and the other categories. While it is far from perfect, OPS has taken major strides toward creating a system of personality typing that is independently verifiable.

To the second point, Ra, like all of us, had a particular set of areas he was naturally good at—his personality preferences—as well as areas where his personality was not as developed. That is all fine and well, but I have found that again and again, he describes living your design as essentially following all of his personality preferences. He is a *significance* guy, in OPS, which is opposite *connection*. Significance people are addicted to feeling special, important, and necessary. They are in touch with what they want. You can tell someone prefers significance over connection if they continually make statements about what they want.

Well, you can imagine what it's like for connection people coming into Human Design. For those who prefer connection (roughly half of the people out there), they are not as in touch with what they want, preferring to be in touch with what other people want. You can imagine what happens when a significance person tells them they are not-self because they aren't in touch enough with what they want. Basically, everyone is going around emulating Ra, not realizing that Ra had a particular set of personality preferences and that no preference is better than any other. Each has its shortcomings. Ra was not a connection guy, and it shows. He had a real problem with connection in his life, making others feel alienated, and often being unable to see things from their perspective. He was stuck in his own solipsistic view of the world, as is common for significance people.

I'm not going to belabor this point because I don't want to get derailed into writing a whole second book on how OPS and Human Design relate to each other. Suffice it to say, in the context of the pseudodiagnosticity bias, Human Design is not the only explanation for much of what it describes, and certainly not the best one. I would urge those who are interested in alternative explanations for much of what Human Design talks about to look into systems like OPS, and other systems of personality typing like the Enneagram of Personality and Attitudinal Psyche. There are a number of great systems of personality typology out there that offer varying degrees of explanatory power in different areas and are worth checking out.

THE OMISSION BIAS

The omission bias is the belief that harmful actions are worse than equally harmful inactions. People may avoid making life changes without permission from a system, perceiving inaction as safer.

For instance, when Human Design says to wait to respond or to wait to be invited, this naturally plays upon what we consider safer. It feels safer not to act than to act, even though inaction can be just as dangerous or even more dangerous at times. But again, we feel it is safer, so a system that tells us not to act has a certain natural validation to it by playing upon our fundamental proclivity for inaction.

THE FOCUSING EFFECT

The focusing effect, or focalism, is putting too much importance on one aspect of an experience or decision. This was described by Schkade and Kahneman in 1998.

We may overemphasize the bodygraph as a central explanation for life outcomes, or we may overemphasize particular decisions that we made as affecting our life more than they really did. By focusing so much on particular things, we ignore the other factors at work.

EMOTIONAL REASONING

Finally, the last cognitive bias we will look at is emotional reasoning, which is believing something is true because it feels true. This is discussed in Cognitive Behavioral Therapy (CBT) literature like that of Aaron Beck and David Burns who describe it as a cognitive distortion. We experience this cognitive distortion any time we feel something carries inherent truth to it without questioning that feeling critically. A big part of CBT is to get enough distance from our emotions by using various emotion-stopping techniques to actually examine our emotions dispassionately. As mentioned before, CBT uses techniques such as reframing the belief we are having an emotion to the belief that we are having a thought that we are having an emotion. Instead of *I feel sad*, I would say to myself, *I am having the thought that I am feeling sad*. This emotional reframing creates a distance from the feeling itself that allows me a potentially necessary space for self-reflection and examination. If I am unable to take that space, I may feel a strong emotional resonance with something, and because of this emotional reaction, take it as evidence that it is true.

As mentioned before, CBT uses emotion-stopping techniques just like Human Design does, and both can be used for good or for ill. There is nothing inherently good or bad about emotion-stopping techniques. They are a tool in the toolbelt. It is a matter of whether we are using that tool to encourage self-reflection and get a safe distance from emotions that would otherwise overwhelm us, or if we are using that same tool to avoid experiencing an emotion that has something to tell us. Hopefully, we can use emotion-stopping techniques wisely, whether from CBT or Human Design.

SUMMARY

We've come a long way in this chapter. We've looked at information processing flaws like confirmation bias and base rate neglect, memory distortions like the hindsight bias, emotional biases like emotional reasoning and the optimism bias, as well as social and identity needs like the Barnum Effect and the egocentric bias. All these biases are a lot to take in, and in truth, each of them is deserving of far more contemplation than the brief overviews here have allowed for. It is my hope that this overview can spark further inquiry, and that different readers will gravitate toward learning more about different biases that speak to them more than others. Each of these cognitive biases tells a story and, in some ways, is an archetype in its own right. If the Barnum Effect most obviously speaks to the quintessential fool archetype, we can see how each of these biases has its own story, although some are easier to see than others. I would urge readers who wish to go deeper into contemplation of the cognitive biases to imagine each bias as an archetypal story that has played out since time immemorial and will continue to play out, at least until such time as humanity evolves past needing to learn its perennial lesson, if that time ever comes.

In the next chapter, we will look at synchronicity and its role in making Human Design compelling.

The essential reality of nature is not separate, self-contained, and complete in itself, so that the human mind can examine it "objectively" and register it from without. Rather, nature's unfolding truth emerges only with the active participation of the human mind. Nature's reality is not merely phenomenal, nor is it independent and objective; rather, it is something that comes into being through the very act of human cognition. Nature becomes intelligible to itself through the human mind.

—Richard Tarnas, *The Passion of the Western Mind*

A synchronistic event is not caused, but it is connected with the meaning of the observer's inner state.

—Marie-Louise von Franz,
Psychological Aspects of the Archetype

It would be most satisfactory if physics and psyche could be seen as complementary aspects of the same reality.

—Wolfgang Pauli, *Atom and Archetype*

Coincidences are spiritual puns. —G. K. Chesterton,
The Mystery of Coincidences

CHAPTER 12: SYNCHRONICITY

IN THIS CHAPTER we will explore Carl Jung's concept of synchronicity and the idea of archetypal synchronistic resonance, a term coined by Jeffrey Mishlove to describe a collection of themes that seem to follow a person.

Jung coined the term synchronicity in the 1920s, defined as meaningful coincidence. Jung did not assume that synchronicities are anything more than coincidences. Indeed, by definition, they are absolutely coincidences. Something that has a clear, deliberate cause cannot be a synchronicity. And yet, Jung's contention is that these coincidences ring out as meaningful in our life. They are significant coincidences. They stand out to us from the background texture of life. *Salient* is a good word here—it means to leap, something that leaps out at us.

It wasn't until 1952 that Jung formalized the notion in his essay *Synchronicity: An Acausal Connecting Principle*, co-authored with Wolfgang Pauli. Incidentally, Pauli was the first to postulate the existence of neutrinos, which play a major role in Human Design cosmology. It was in this 1952 work that Jung formulated synchronicity as a principle that connects the inner and outer worlds, psyche and matter. He called this linkage an acausal connecting principle. It's acausal—there is no cause. Remember, by definition, it's a coincidence. If there were a cause then it wouldn't be a coincidence. Yet, there is a connecting principle at work. Inner and outer life is connected in some way.

Jung and Pauli were avid friends and collaborators who attempted to develop an understanding of reality as what they called dual aspect substance monism, which is a fancy way of saying that psyche and matter are two parts of the same thing. Pauli conjectured there may be a symbolic framework that prefigures both psyche and matter.

The term synchronicity refers to any coincidence that takes on special significance. It is a coincidence. There is no causal orderedness at this level, such as we would find in a causal chain of events. And yet Jung felt there must still be an order at work. The synchronistic event gives the subjective experience of glimpsing at a divine order hidden behind the appearance of things. It seems as though there is some hidden purpose, some great mystery being revealed, but only in glimpses.

Jung was interested in a number of paranormal and unscientific or mystical fields. He arranged séances, studied alchemical and mystical texts, and was fascinated by astrology. At one point, working with Dr. F. J. Jaff, the statistician, Jung analyzed over 400 couples looking for particular astrological configurations that might indicate couplehood.

In his first statistical analysis, although it was quite small by scientific standards, he nevertheless found promising evidence that astrological aspects had some predictive capacity for whether two people would marry. Later, he expanded his sample size and the effect went away. Jung concluded that it was a synchronicity.

The first sample set presented a compelling coincidence. It was a statistically anomalous pattern that suggested more than randomness, but it went away when the sample size was increased, showing itself to have actually been random all along.

He took these types of statistical anomalies as meaningful coincidences, which he would go on to refer to as evidence for an acausal connecting principle or acausal orderedness. As mentioned, this is about seeing symbolic parallels between inner psychological states and outer events. This is something different from causality or probability. It's not that astrology was causing anything, nor that it was changing the probabilities beyond randomness and mere chance. It was simply the fact that his inner psychic realities paralleled outer events. These parallels were fascinating to Jung.

Jung also began I Ching experiments. He believed divinatory systems like the I Ching worked not through causal mechanisms, but because of subjective parallels in moments of heightened meaning, especially under states of psychological duress or excitement. This was one explanation for why they could not be reproduced in laboratory settings. If a particular heightened state of psychological intensity was required, the sterile laboratory environment was not going to reproduce such events.

From Jung's essay *Synchronicity: An Acausal Connecting Principle*, Jung says: "A statistically significant result may be only a hint, a suggestion, not a proof for the individual." However, despite ack of proof, this hint or suggestion may be still be transformative.

To me, Jung offers a third path in understanding how things like astrology and Human Design work. If the first path is the belief in a causal mechanism behind Human Design, and the second path is the belief that cognitive biases are the only mechanism at work, this third path admits there may not be a causal mechanism, and admits that we have cognitive biases, but goes beyond that to raise the question of whether mystical systems actually function through synchronicity.

We may have an inner psychological reality that finds a parallel in the language or descriptions of the system. From this perspective, it's less about your Human Design bodygraph truly describing aspects of your biological or energetic makeup and more about the language used having some resonant, synchronistic effect connected to your inner experience.

It's essentially saying that Human Design is invalid in the way that it claims to be, and yet it is still valid or potentially valid in another way. Ra was wrong when he said that your time of birth dictates your energetic blueprint and that there are such a thing as types, centers, lines, and the rest of it. But even though he was wrong about that, the system itself still somehow works. And the question is, how does it work?

In pondering this question, I thought about bibliomancy— how you can open up a book to any random page and choose any random word on that page. It may, although there is no guarantee, have some relation to your own internal state. It's the same with tarot cards. You can draw a card and it might point to an internal state.

If you are unable to make the connection, you can either seek to understand the card a little better, adding what Jung called amplification—drawing connections between that card and certain life themes—or you can draw another card. By the time you've amplified a single card with a few connections or added a few more cards, a picture begins to emerge.

While we can explain away that picture as apophenia, no different than seeing faces in clouds, perhaps Jung gives us a way of appreciating why this process may actually have value.

Arthur Koestler, author of *The Roots of Coincidence* (1972), proposes that synchronicity may play a role in scientific discoveries, that synchronicity typically occurs during creative breakthroughs. It would make sense that a creative breakthrough is a period of high psychological excitement or tension as well.

If synchronicities do actually happen more frequently at some times and not others, it basically amounts to saying sometimes people are luckier than others. This is a pretty bizarre idea since there is not really any scientific basis for a notion like luck. The fact that a gambler might win a lot on one night and lose a lot on the next night is attributed to random chance. And yet, what Jung was finding is that there may actually be clusters of events that are somehow connected. They just aren't connected causally and they do not violate the laws of chance.

Koestler gathered stories from scientists showing something similar. For instance, Kekulé's dream of the benzene ring was crucial in advancing the field of biological chemistry. Koestler found that scientists often had dreams or other synchronistic occurrences that somehow corresponded to their breakthroughs.

Another interesting thought he had is that biological evolution itself may happen rather synchronistically, which is to say coincidentally. This is an interesting question deserving of further thought because synchronicities are by definition meaningful, so this would seem to imply that meaning is involved in the evolutionary process. The usual approach to the question of how meaning arises ascribes it solely to humans, as something that has no basis outside of human experience. Perhaps other mammals have some sort of proto-meaning making but the idea we usually encounter is that humans are creating meaning every step of the way. Humans are the meaning makers.

Archetypal astrologer Richard Tarnas has a book of astro-history, if we can call it that, called *Cosmos and Psyche* (2006). He tells the story of the last 500 years of Western history through the lens of astrology and makes a compelling story using the archetypal themes of outer planetary transits. He makes a great case for major world events having symbolic parallels to the themes expressed by the planetary transits.

Uranus goes conjunct with Pluto on average every 140 years. It goes conjunct with Neptune around every 170 years. If you look at the theme of Uranus as revolution, innovation, technological upheaval and breakthrough, we should have periods of great revolution during these conjunctions. With Pluto, this breakthrough could be violent, volcanic, eruptive, destructive, obsessive, and other Plutonic themes. With Neptune, it would take on the quality of the archetypal dream world, the plenum and pleroma— Neptune is, in some sense, the archetype of the archetypal field itself, the maya, the world as illusion and play of forces. Sure enough, our last Uranus-Pluto conjunction occurred in the mid-1960s during a time of great upheaval, and Uranus-Neptune happened around the time of the advent of the Internet in the early 1990s.

Tarnas does not claim that the planetary cycles cause earthly events to happen. He seems to follow Jung in the belief that there is an acausal orderedness connecting things beyond the mechanisms of cause-and-effect. There are something like inbuilt tendencies where different orders tend to express the same symbolic information.

Here we get to something close to Mishlove's idea of archetypal synchronistic resonance (ASR). Mishlove's idea was developed in part to explain, or at least explore, some of the interesting findings of past life researchers. Essentially, one of the ways people end up thinking they have found evidence for reincarnation is a number of coincidences that connect a person to someone else who lived and died before in history. There is no way to prove reincarnation, let alone that someone alive today is the reincarnation of someone who lived before, but these coincidences are nevertheless compelling, and those who study past lives may be convinced by them. The skeptics among us will likely point out that there are countless aspects of a person's life that do not have any connection whatsoever to the historical figure—that the coincidences are cherry-picked. If someone has 10 or 12 coincidences linking them to a historical figure, why should we include those and ignore the countless other aspects of a person's life that have no connection to that figure? And yet, despite the cries of skeptics, there is something compelling about these coincidences. They may not be evidence of past lives, but they certainly seem to be evidence of something—the question is just, what are they evidence of?

Again, for Jung, they are evidence of what he calls acausal orderedness, a connecting principle that reveals a hidden order of things beyond causal order. It seems to me we have a redemptive method available here. We can redeem much of the value of fields like Human Design and astrology if we take the right tack in approaching them. For Jung, and I agree wholeheartedly, the danger is in taking things too literally and becoming possessed by an archetypal complex. We will explore archetypes in the next chapter, but the basic idea here is that we can get a lot of value from synchronistic systems: tarot, I Ching, astrology, Human Design or any system which produces potentially meaningful statements about us and our conditions. We just have to interpret that information as a sort of synchronistic feedback, or synchronistic resonance. If we fail to interpret the information correctly, we become overly identified with it, sometimes to the point where we completely lose our old identity. We suffer what Jung calls an inflation, where we become inflated with transpersonal "energy"—themes, ideas, archetypal values. We lose ourselves and, while we may gain a rush from the influx of the transpersonal, even to the point of having a mystical-religious experience, there is a great danger here. We will explore the idea of archetypes and the dangers of archetypal possession in the next chapter.

CHAPTER 13: ARCHETYPES

THE NOTION OF ARCHETYPES is highly useful in understanding the mechanisms behind why something like astrology or Human Design is so convincing. There has to be some psychic energy behind it, some weight or power to captivate us. And it is the archetypes, also known as the archetypal complexes, which have this power.

There are many approaches to understanding archetypes. One approach is to assume that there are archetypes and non-archetypal phenomena. In this view, archetypal phenomena are those that fit into relatively clearly defined symbolic parameters—archetypal roles like mother and father, or archetypal stories like the hero's journey. Non-archetypal phenomena would be more singular. They do not fit into any category. They are not an archetype of anything other than perhaps being an archetype of themselves. This is an approach which basically divides things into whether they belong to an archetypal category, or whether they are anomalous. That is the first approach.

Or—and this is my preference—we can interpret archetypes as all-encompassing. That is, there is nothing which does not have an archetype. I much prefer this totalizing view, because then even the attempt to escape the archetype is itself archetypal.

It's like the great Bill Hicks joke, where in his stand-up routine he talks about how much he despises marketers. Then he imagines there are some marketers in the audience saying, "Ooh, that's really good, Bill. Go after that anti-marketing dollar. That's a big dollar."

It's sort of like capitalism. If capitalism is truly all-encompassing, then even anti-capitalism becomes a form of capitalism. It's subsumed by it. If everyone is selling something, then even the attempt to sell nothing is still selling something—it's selling the anti-capitalist shtick.

This is how I like to think of archetypes. An archetype is essentially a symbolic assemblage of images, ideas, emotions, and anything else that can be connected. It's basically a pattern. Even the attempt to have no pattern is still a pattern. You can pattern-match all the different patterns and then arrive at a new meta-pattern, which is "no pattern at all." It's like having a box to put each thing in, and then the things that don't fit into any box go into their own box. It's all boxes.

I like this approach. I'm not saying it's the only way to imagine archetypes. We could also systematize them in a way that isn't totalizing—a way that does allow for a distinction between the archetypal and the non-archetypal. But I prefer to see it all as archetypal. In my worldview, everything is archetypal.

What does this worldview do? It gives us a lens for analyzing things according to the interconnections and patterns that link them with each other. It gives things connective tissue.

I don't think archetypes can ever be fully clearly defined, nor can they ever encompass entirely exclusive domains. They're all partially overlapping. A single idea may fit into twenty different archetypes. In that sense, archetypes are highly contextual. The same idea may fit into the hero archetype, but also into the villain archetype. What we're really getting into here are deep questions about categories, models, beliefs, ideas, and—funny enough—images.

The post-Jungian theorist James Hillman distanced himself from Jung, finding Jung too conceptual, and argued for the primacy of images. Meanwhile, Jacques Derrida, the founder of the philosophical school of deconstruction, explored similar areas of thought such as the entanglement of concept and image.

So much of philosophy is easily framed as trying to win in a competition of symbols—to defeat the opponent and cast one's own worldview into the supreme position. Even Derrida, that great detractor of grand narratives, created his own grand narrative: the anti-narrative, or no narrative. The same could be said of François Laruelle, who developed what he called non-philosophy as an attempt to reject the philosophical stance that elevates itself above all others. And yet, in rejecting philosophy, he framed himself as the great philosopher—so great, in fact, that he didn't do philosophy at all. He did non-philosophy. You can see how such postures are always positioning themselves as the real thing against all the other attempts that ostensibly don't get it.

In any case, I prefer seeing things through the lens of archetypes because it gives us a language for describing worldviews, philosophies, and much else. It offers a vocabulary for describing aspects of these worldviews that might not otherwise be apparent.

Returning to *Cosmos and Psyche*, which we discussed in the previous chapter, the question becomes: how do we see the world through the lens of archetypes, and what does this worldview give us? Does seeing world events as archetypal clusters give us a benefit over seeing them through a merely causal lens? Can we deduce any deeper truths about the nature of reality, or is it better to stay away from conjectures as to what it means? This latter idea arises because it is all too easy to read deep meanings into synchronicities, only to later have those meanings called into question. Indeed, isn't much of the problem with building up a system of beliefs around synchronistic occurrences that we then close ourselves off to further interpretive action, believing we've already found the truth?

Regardless of whether Tarnas' highly compelling narrative of history is entirely synchronistic, which is to say, coincidental—and I actually believe it is—it may still be a valid and invigorating way of approaching world history that gets us to see hidden resonances between chance occurrences. That's worth something.

And yet, I also believe we could likely find just as compelling examples of synchronistic resonance without relying on his presupposition that astrological cycles provide the only valid lens. Of course there is something compelling about the cycles of the planets. They are facts. We know when the planets are aligned—we have telescopes that can prove this fact. My question is whether we would find just as much archetypal synchronistic resonance if we do away with the reliance on planetary cycles altogether. In fact, I tried doing exactly that: picking arbitrary dates and arbitrary archetypal themes. And it actually worked.

I don't really think his book proves the validity of astrology any more than it proves that any chosen archetypal themes will be found to match global events that occur within a purely arbitrary period. I do really enjoy Tarnas' storytelling ability, and I also enjoy the question he raises around meaning. I am just not entirely convinced that the archetypal themes associated with the planets occur more during major planetary alignments than otherwise.

The value, to me, is in raising some big questions about the nature of reality, belief, and meaning. Tarnas basically asks: Is meaning something that humans create, or is it part of reality itself—reality outside of humans—the same reality studied by physicists, biologists, astronomers, and others in the hard sciences?

What Tarnas says here is fascinating. He argues that humanity has been moving beyond layer after layer of hubris. In ancient times, we thought we were the center of the cosmos and that everything revolved around us. The Copernican Revolution shattered that. We learned that we go around the sun. Then Darwin showed us that we weren't created by God but evolved from apes. Later, Freud revealed that we aren't even masters of our own minds. The unconscious coexists with us, shaping our behavior in ways we don't control. We don't even have dominion over our internal subjective reality.

But Tarnas suggests that the last great bastion of hubris is around meaning itself: *the idea that we are the sole arbiters of meaning in an otherwise meaningless cosmos*, in his words—that meaning is just something humans project onto an indifferent universe. Tarnas argues that we must overcome this belief and recognize that meaning, purpose, and morality are embedded in the very fabric of reality. They are not human inventions. We've simply claimed them in our hubris as though they belonged to us. You can see how this is a pretty controversial perspective in most philosophical circles.

The philosopher Ray Brassier, in his book *Nihil Unbound* (2007), essentially presents a nihilist manifesto. He argues that all meaning is applied retroactively—that things first appear meaningless, and only later, through a process of understanding and narrative construction, do we ascribe meaning to them. Then he brings in cosmology. It is a known fact that the entire universe will eventually wind down into the so-called heat death of the universe. All stars will burn out, all life will be extinguished, and the universe will become shrouded in eternal darkness. Brassier claims that this means, through the process of retroactive signification, that ultimately anything that has any meaning whatsoever will eventually become meaningless.

I have a lot of problems with this argument. How pompous to think he knows what the future holds, that he alone sees the truth of the meaninglessness of reality, as if the rest of the philosophers hadn't thoroughly considered this viewpoint already and found it lacking. Brassier presents himself as the only philosopher alive who can face the abhorrent truth of the utter meaninglessness of existence, and he presents this maneuver as the ultimate overcoming of hubris. In other words, Tarnas is saying that our great hubris is thinking that we create meaning, when really meaning exists independently of us. Brassier is saying that our great hubris is thinking that meaning exists at all—anything more than a fleeting delusion in the addled brains of domesticated primates.

In response to Brassier, I like Quentin Meillassoux's thought experiment. Meillassoux agrees with Brassier that retroactive signification is how meaning works, but he proposes that even after the potential heat death of the universe, there could be a later time in which everything that came before is reframed. There could be an eternal afterlife where we're all sitting around laughing, drinking tea. We really don't know. At any point, something could happen that changes everything that came before in the extreme. Meillassoux calls this hyper-chaos. He says that our normal understanding of change is that A becomes B. But hyper-chaos is when A becomes B so fully that it was never A in the first place. It was only A temporarily, before it changed to B, at which point the change was so complete that it retroactively erased the fact that it was ever A. It was always B all along.

Without going too deep into these philosophical speculations, I'll simply say that this is a rich area of study—the intersection of meaning-making, belief, reality, and occurrences in the world, and how they interact with each other. The most I can say is that our awareness and beliefs interact with events happening in reality, and that this interaction cannot be reduced to either one or the other outcome. It isn't true to say that beliefs exclusively create reality, nor is it true to say that reality creates beliefs. It's an admixture of both.

Bringing it back to the original topic, I believe the study of synchronicity and the role of archetypes offers a kind of middle ground for those who don't wish to fully accept that Human Design is "real," nor fully reject it as being entirely false. It may be false at the level of scientific fact, and yet there may be a mechanism within reality—acausal orderedness—that still makes systems like Human Design have psychological relevance. Despite the lack of a causal mechanism, Human Design and other synchronistic-archetypal systems may actually help people.

It's hard for me to say whether Human Design helped me or not. It certainly seems like it both helped and harmed, but I can't say to what extent.

What I can say is that there were so many synchronicities at various times in my Human Design journey that it certainly seemed highly relevant. Perhaps one of the problems is that I didn't interpret these synchronicities as what they were. I interpreted them as evidence that Human Design was real, when a better interpretation would simply be to take them as evidence of a parallel reflection of my internal state. Instead of reading too much into them or taking them too seriously, perhaps I could have simply accepted that they got me onto a new line of thought or a different approach. Perhaps I could have embraced the creative breakthrough without the detrimental rigid beliefs.

Why had I taken them too seriously? Why had I interpreted these synchronistic occurrences as evidence of the reality of Human Design? Here, I defer back to Dr. Robert Moore's description of the archetypes which we explored in Chapter 9. Moore describes the archetypes as radioactive, contagious, and possessive. Here, perhaps we ought to speak of archetypal complexes, and remember that Jung coined this term, complex, which is now part of our modern colloquial vernacular: *he has a mother complex, she has a superiority complex, they have an inferiority complex*. In fact, Jung first called his offshoot of psychoanalysis by the name complex psychology, not in the sense that it is complicated, but that it is the psychology of the complexes. The whole idea of the complex acting on a person is really the same thing as being possessed by, or identifying with an archetype. Archetypal possession and identification may not be exactly identical, depending how the terms are used—the first can mean an entirely unconscious identification, while sometimes the claim of identification with a complex implies some level of conscious awareness. But, I would point out that identification can be entirely unconscious, and in most usages, these terms are interchangeable.

It seems to me that any time we take synchronistic events too seriously, it is because we have come to identify with and be possessed by certain archetypal contents. Something has captivated us, whether we imagine that thing as an idea, belief, image, or story. We have become infected by it, so to speak, and, having caught the virus, we cannot stop thinking about it. We see it everywhere. We have been seduced by it. We have given ourselves over to something outside of us—impersonal and imperialistic—through connecting with that numinous energy coming off these things (Moore's words). We have been taken over by the enormous seductive power of the archetype that has the ability to overwhelm the critical powers of the ego (Moore's words again).

This is what Jung understood, and what we must come to understand when exploring such questions of how cultic qualities can emerge. Before we exert control on ourselves or others, we are first controlled by the archetypal complex. We identify with something that begins to inform our thoughts, beliefs and behavior. Only when we break free from identification with the archetypal complex can we regain our critical thinking abilities.

There is a real problem here. By remaining aloof, skeptical, overly tied to our critical thinking abilities, we do not allow ourselves to enter into engagement with the fullness of what it means to be alive—the full range of human experience, which involves actually experiencing the magic and synchronicity of life. And yet, there is a real danger in those experiences. We are tested by them.

Many people will remain so skeptical of the magical, mystical, religious, spiritual and imaginal realms (to borrow a term from Henry Corbin) that they never open themselves up to the range of human experience available to us all. They remain trapped in a small version of reality. They do not develop fully as people because of a fear, however justified, of the dangers of opening themselves up to these archetypal forces. Others will open themselves up to the dangers of the archetypes and be tested. Whether they come out the other side of that experience or end up succumbing to the dangers of the archetypes is something that can only be determined by the complex interaction of their innate psychological resources and, in some part, the winds of fate. It is a complex interaction of nature, nurture, and singular force of will, plus a lot of chance events. Each of us must decide for ourselves whether we will play it safe in life, remaining tethered to a skepticism that protects us from archetypal invasion, or whether we will explore the mysteries and open ourselves up. There is a real risk involved, and also a real reward. The risk is not for nothing.

It would be too easy if all we had to do was remain staunchly skeptical. If our task as humans was merely to keep ourselves from being tricked, to overcome magical thinking, to remain firmly entrenched in the materialist-rational view of the world, our job would have been finished ages ago. We would have been done already with the Enlightenment and the advent of the sciences. No, our task is far more difficult than that. We must exist within the tension between the protective faculties of critical thinking and the archetypal-imaginal realms of the mysteries of life. The archetypes are, if nothing else, invigorating. They are life-bringing. They have a vitalizing effect. All it takes is to think of those times we have been in love—itself an archetypal experience—to realize how different life can be during such times of heightened psychological experience. We cannot live without some level of energy from the archetypes. To be free of all archetypal energy is to be devoid of energy, period. It is to be a walking corpse, a zombie. It seems our lot in life as humans on this plane is to exist with the double bind: we can't live with archetypal complexes possessing us, and we can't live without them. Some level of possession is vitalizing. Too much is annihilating.

We have arrived at the perennial wisdom that medicine and poison are the same thing in different doses and at different times. A dose of magic and mystery may be just the right thing to cure us of the doldrums of mundane life. It may cure our ennui. A dose of scientific rationalism and critical thinking may snap us out of a trance-like identification with an archetypal complex that is no longer energizing us, but actually draining our energy. It may free our attention from being fully trapped in obsessive captivation, or what Lacan called *captation* to describe a particular way that images can catch hold of the psyche and hold us captive to them.

Living a full life seems to require a certain freedom of thought and movement to allow for both medicines to be administered when needed, and to know which is needed in any given phase.

They are themselves part of the very reality that they recognize as conflictual and antagonistic. In such a case the criterion of scientific objectivity is not supposed neutrality, but the capacity of theory to occupy a singular, specific point of view within the situation. [...] One cannot see everything from everywhere; some positions dissimulate the conflict, and some reveal it.
—Alenka Zupančič, *Why Psychoanalysis?*

Modern science, in its devotion to measurable and quantifiable phenomena, often fails to recognize the reality of the inner psychic domain, not because it does not exist, but because it cannot be measured by conventional means.
—Richard Tarnas, *Cosmos and Psyche*

The psychic life cannot be observed in the sense of an external experiment; it can only be experienced, and the evidence is experiential, not statistical.
—Marie-Louise von Franz,
Psychological Aspects of the Archetype

CHAPTER 14: ATTEMPTS AT SCIENTIFIC

VALIDATION

As WE GET TO THE END of this book, I'd like to review a few of my own personal attempts to validate the Human Design System.

It is a commonplace in Human Design that it's all an experiment that you should validate for yourself. Well, that sounds great in theory, but how many people actually have the means, resources, or energy to validate something using a more scientific approach? Very few.

The idea of validation in Human Design has more to do with seeing for yourself. It is framed as testing how following strategy and authority impacts your own life by trying it out and seeing the results. If you don't see results, just keep waiting. It takes time. At least, that's what I was told for many years in my initial investigations in the system. What ends up happening is that this urge to keep experimenting can function as a mechanism to keep people engaged with the system far longer than they otherwise would. It's basically a way of saying, suspend your judgment, suspend your disbelief. Wait for seven years. Then we can talk.

Instead of just experimenting personally, I took this idea of experimenting in a scientific sense. I devised several attempts to validate certain statements made by Ra Uru Hu. This was not an easy task, not least because Ra made many statements that are wholly unfalsifiable. First, I had to find statements made by Ra that could actually be tested.

How do you validate the claim that following your strategy and authority leads to "satisfaction"? Sure, you could interview people in the Human Design community about their happiness levels, but you'd be relying entirely on self-report. That might get you an idea of how much people claim to have a high happiness level, but it doesn't get at causal factors. Besides, self-report is notoriously unreliable within high-control belief systems, where a major aspect of the control is shaping what adherents believe about themselves.

This raises an obvious problem: how do we know the system isn't simply self-selecting for those who are already inclined toward believing it works, and that this belief itself ensures positive self-reporting? With that in mind, I focused on statements from Ra that were actually testable.

I first began looking at statements Ra made about astronomical subjects. One such claim Ra made is that Sirius A has already gone supernova but we haven't seen it yet because the light hasn't reached us. Ra made that statement in 2006. Sirius A is only 8.6 light-years away. If it had gone supernova, we would absolutely know by now. That's a statement that can be unequivocally proven false.

I began looking for other claims I could test. Here's a short list of some of the claims I found along with my fact checking:

Ra's Claim	Fact Check
Sirius A went supernova but the light hasn't reached us yet.	Sirius A is only 8.6 light-years away. If it had gone supernova, we would already know.
50% of people have the same color on the personality and design sides; the other 50% have different personality and design colors.	Actually, it's around 24.59% of people who have the same color on both sides, and the other 75.41% have different colors.
Base changes every few seconds, making it nearly impossible to obtain an accurate calculation from birth records.	*Base* changes roughly every 7 and a half minutes. (It does change every few *arcseconds,* however, which is a measure of space, not time, perhaps leading to Ra's confusion.)
The Voice told Ra that neutrinos have mass. When it was proven they have mass, it validated Ra's encounter.	Beginning in the 1950s, and increasingly in the 1960s and 1970s, several scientists predicted that neutrinos might have mass.
Type was validated scientifically through statistical analysis.	Ra never predicted type percentages or even mentioned type. Once he came up with the criteria of type, a statistical analysis was performed which found the distribution of these categories, but that does not prove the existence of type.
Base 1 people are 90% likely to be male; *base 3* are 90% likely to be female. It is rare to find base 1 females or base 3 males.	A statistical analysis of over 5,000 bodygraphs found no statistical correlation.

Some of these erroneous claims made by Ra can be chalked up to honest mistakes. He obviously didn't realize that base changes every seven and a half minutes when he said repeatedly it changes every few seconds. He may have been honestly confused about what constitutes evidence when he claimed the concept of type was scientifically validated. In other cases, he seems to have just made guesses or wrong assumptions. In the case of saying that the Voice told him neutrinos have mass, that seems a little more disingenuous, because he could have easily fact-checked that others said this for decades. He was also a little disingenuous in failing to mention that the actual wheel sequence of the hexagrams in the *rave mandala* had been around for centuries.

When I first began studying Human Design, I had endless questions about how it might connect to other systems and whether it could be scientifically validated. I posted questions in prominent online groups at the time, and was promptly shut down.

The replies were a litany of thinly disguised insults dressed as Human Design analysis: "Do you have an Undefined Head? You're thinking about things that don't matter." "Do you have an Undefined Ego? You seem like you're trying to prove some-thing." "Do you have an Undefined Throat? Why are you trying to get attention?" "Are you a Generator? Then why are you initi-ating by making these posts?"

Over time, I stopped sharing my questions and I stopped telling people about the experiments I wanted to do, but I remained curious. One of my first curiosities was whether Human Design correlated in any way with personality type theory, for example, Jung's four-function model. I eventually concluded that it does not. There are numerous documented cases of twins born seconds apart who have different personality types but identical Human Design bodygraphs. To me, that demonstrates that the bodygraph cannot predict personality type.

But I had many other questions as well. I wanted to know whether Human Design could be proven scientifically. Ra himself made numerous claims that Human Design was a science and that his claims had been scientifically proven. When neutrinos were discovered to have mass in 1998, Ra made a big deal about how this supposedly validated Human Design. He even swapped his mystic kufi for a baseball cap, claiming this was his nod to science, that he was no longer a mystic. He asserted that the Voice had told him neutrinos have mass before it was scientifically proven. In reality, the hypothesis that neutrinos have mass dates back to the 1950s.

Another claim Ra made is that his concept of type was scientifically validated. He cited research by Eleanor and Marvin Haspel-Portner, who analyzed thousands of birth times and recorded the distribution of types. Ra claimed that the observed distributions matched what the Voice had told him.

A later study in 2008, conducted with Adrian Kobler, found similar type distributions. Ra argued this proved the validity of type, because if type weren't real, the argument goes, there wouldn't be consistent averages. But this isn't actually how statistics work. You could define arbitrary types based on any combination of the bodygraph—say, *people with a Defined Solar Plexus and Defined Spleen*—and you'd still get consistent percentages.

One claim in particular stood out to me as easy to test. In Human Design, everyone supposedly belongs to one of five bases. Your base comes from two numbers, one from your personality calculation at the time of birth and one from your design date.

Ra claimed that about 90% of people with base 1 are male, and similarly, 90% of people with base 3 are female. He also claimed this was unprovable at the time because accurate birth data wasn't available, but that some future generation could verify it.

It turns out that it isn't that hard to test this claim. I used the Astro-Databank, a database containing thousands of birth records. I wasn't able to obtain their full dataset, but I was able to get a subset of around 6,000 records with the highest accuracy rating ("AA," meaning birth certificate in hand). I calculated the base for each of these individuals and checked whether there was any correlation with assigned sex at birth.

The result? No correlation whatsoever.

For base 1, Ra had predicted 90% male. In fact, there were 17 fewer males than expected, but this is a negligible deviation within the range of pure chance for a dataset of that size. For base 3, where Ra predicted 90% female, there were 6 more females than expected—again, statistically insignificant. I had conclusively demonstrated that Ra's claim was false.

Of all claims I was able to test, four were outright false, and two—neutrino mass and Type distribution—were examples of Ra misunderstanding or misrepresenting what was really going on there. He failed to mention that he was not the first to predict neutrino mass, and either misunderstood or misrepresented his supposed evidence for Type distribution.

Ra also misunderstood basic technical details. As mentioned, he claimed we could never determine someone's Base with accuracy because it changes every few seconds. This is seemingly a confusion between seconds of arc (a spatial measurement used in astrology) and seconds of time.

The reality is, there aren't very many testable claims in Human Design. Most of what Ra says can only be evaluated through qualitative methods like interviews or questionnaires, which are fraught with confirmation bias, placebo effects, and groupthink.

Nevertheless, I tried to think of ways that more rigorous testing might be done. One idea came from my earlier attempts to validate the claims of Richard Tarnas in *Cosmos and Psyche*. Tarnas claims that key points in outer planet synodic cycles (like Uranus–Pluto conjunctions) correlate with major historical events that reflect specific archetypal themes. For example, the Uranus–Pluto conjunction of the 1960s lines up with technological and political revolutions.

To test this, I took a list of Uranus–Pluto conjunctions, squares, and oppositions and looked at three-year windows surrounding each. Sure enough, significant historical events matching the themes occurred. But then I moved those windows forward by 10 years, back by 10 years, forward by 15 years, and the same thing happened. I could always find world events that matched the supposed archetypal themes. In fact, sometimes the random dates lined up even better than the "correct" ones. I concluded that you can find archetypal events matching planetary themes pretty much any time. This is the nature of how humans impose pattern recognition onto chaotic data.

A similar approach could be taken with Human Design's transit predictions or global cycle analysis. You could pick time windows unrelated to Human Design's predictions and find events that fit the supposed archetypal themes just as well.

As for experiments testing individual Human Design claims, most would require large-scale, longitudinal studies. For example, does following strategy and authority lead to greater satisfaction, success, peace, or surprise? You'd need to track thousands of people over years while rigorously controlling for biases.

Even then, believers would likely dismiss the results. If the data showed no benefit, defenders would say, "Well, Human Design doesn't promise happiness—just the life you're designed for." But this is disingenuous. Ra repeatedly claimed that following Human Design leads to better outcomes, including less resistance, better relationships, improved health, and psychological satisfaction. This retreat into ambiguity is another thought-terminating cliché. It halts all further critical inquiry.

There are many specific claims that could be tested:

Do people with Emotional Authority make better decisions when they wait, compared to those with Sacral Authority who respond in the moment?

Do Projectors experience greater success when they wait for invitations versus when they don't?

Do Reflectors genuinely experience stronger mood variability based on lunar transits?

Does a Defined Spleen correlate with greater intuition?

Does a Defined Ego correlate with willpower, self-discipline, or delay of gratification?

You could even conduct blinded tests. For instance, give Human Design analysts life narratives and see if they can correctly guess someone's Incarnation Cross based on the story of their life. I suspect the results would be no better than chance.

But here's the deeper problem: any time an experiment like this is proposed, defenders of the system move the goalposts. They claim that nothing is guaranteed, that these are just tendencies, not certainties. If that's true, then the predictive power of the body-graph collapses into vagueness.

I also thought about testing the Emotional Center by examining whether those with a Defined Solar Plexus exhibit detectable emotional waves, while those without do not. Similarly, the claim that non-sacral types experience burnout from 9-to-5 jobs could be tested by measuring physiological markers like cortisol and heart rate variability. Anecdotally, I've met just as many burnt-out sacral types as non-sacrals.

Frankly, I believe that psychological models like Objective Personality—which tracks behavioral patterns related to energy management—explain burnout far better than anything in the Human Design chart.

Ra often claimed that Human Design is not a belief system but a mechanical one. You could test that, too. Assign random charts to people and compare whether they report the same benefits as those using their "correct" charts. This would reveal how much of Human Design's efficacy is placebo.

Many other tests are possible. You could examine whether split definition people really seek out others who bridge their splits.

You could check whether specific profiles cluster in certain professions more than chance would predict, for example, if there are more people who have the 5/1 profile in leadership roles.

But the truth is, I haven't bothered to carry out most of these experiments. Why? Because I'm convinced it would be a tremendous amount of work with very little payoff.

To me, it's clear that Human Design operates as a psychological inkblot. People project meaning onto it, find value in the process of self-reflection, and sometimes gain insight. But the belief that the bodygraph itself holds any objective, scientific truth? I see no evidence for that at all.

Philosophy, which pretends to enunciate the Truth of things once and for all, embodies this paradoxical characteristic of being, in its essence, conflictual, and perpetually so.
—Louis Althusser, *Philosophy and the Spontaneous Philosophy of the Scientists*

Being is a becoming because, by continually rotating, it never stands still, neither advances nor regresses despite always moving. No point on the rotating circumference can be a stage of time's progress. There are no phases, no advances, no regression, since the wheel's rotation always returns it to the same point.
—James Hillman, *Alchemical Psychology*

Life is a series of natural and spontaneous changes. Don't resist them - that only creates sorrow. Let reality be reality. Let things flow naturally forward in whatever way they like.
—Lao Tzu, *Tao Te Ching*

It shows an excessive tenderness for the world to remove contradiction from it and then to transfer the contradiction to reason, where it is allowed to remain unresolved.
—G. W. F. Hegel, *Science of Logic*

If the world weren't such a beautiful place, we might all turn into cynics. —Paul Auster, *Moon Palace*

CHAPTER 15: CLOSING REMARKS

IF SOMEONE HAD TOLD ME ONE YEAR AGO that I would be writing this book, I would have said they were crazy. I never imagined there was such a thing for me as life after Human Design.

I had such a strong, irrational confidence that with Human Design, I had found my life's purpose. I believed I was put on this planet to preserve Human Design knowledge and help others by sharing that knowledge. I looked to the many synchronicities in my life as indicators that I was on the right path—including, as mentioned, moving to Santa Fe and buying a home only a quarter mile from Genoa Bliven, the director of Human Design America, and his partner and collaborator Lasita Shalev. Meeting them and undergoing mentorship from them was an incredible experience and one I am genuinely grateful for. I consider them close friends who have been supportive every step of the way in my journey. They have both been a great source of wisdom and insight into life's inner workings, something that I attribute to their own innate qualities as human beings, and not something that can be explained as being caused in any way by Human Design.

I've met so many wonderful people in the Human Design community. Perhaps my greatest fear in writing this book is that I might insult them in some way. Just as I hoped those I care about in the Human Design community would not judge me for leaving, I also don't want them to feel judged. It was difficult for me to go from an extreme, fanatical belief in the validity of Human Design to an equally extreme rejection of it—coming to see it as a cult. I hope that as I've processed this new perspective, I've landed somewhere closer to a middle ground. I don't want to swing from being fanatically pro–Human Design to being fanatically anti–Human Design.

The truth is, Human Design probably does help a lot of people. I've wrestled with my own involvement. I've asked myself hard questions, like whether it's ethical to continue having hundreds of hours of Human Design material available for free on my YouTube channel. Should I keep it available online? Is it unethical of me to perpetuate Human Design? Or would it be more unethical to try to control other people's interest in it by removing the videos, simply because I no longer subscribe to those beliefs?

For years, I worked long hours, pretty much for free. I used to say there are things you do to make money, and there are things you make money to do—and Human Design was something I made money to do. Some prominent figures in the Human Design world—people making hundreds of thousands of dollars per year—told me I was crazy not to monetize my teaching more. While I did make a small amount of money, I spent nearly every penny on Human Design projects: buying rare tapes and CDs for the Santa Fe Human Design Library (SFHDL) that I founded, or purchasing gifts for attendees at the HDHD conference each year. I would max out my credit cards trying to outdo the previous year with extra perks for participants.

I was such a fanatical believer that I didn't put much thought into my own financial compensation. I saw the work I was doing as its own reward.

At the end of the day, I came to the conclusion that my conscience is okay with having my former teachings available. If there's anything out there that no longer feels right to me, I will remove it. But for the most part, I do feel comfortable keeping those materials online.

As for the organizations I started—the Center for Human Design, High Desert Human Design, the Santa Fe Human Design Library, and others—I will either be closing them down or handing them off to friends and colleagues I trust, people that I know will carry on with the mission in a way that doesn't perpetuate the more cultic aspects, like high control or high demand. Thankfully, I have friends in the community who I am confident won't fall into those patterns.

For myself, I feel an overwhelming sense of relief no longer holding myself to such a strict level of scrutiny. Even making a statement like "I feel" would have been something I previously scrutinized. In Ra's material on the Voices of the Throat Center, he describes how each of us has certain voices that are authentic and others that are not-self. According to the system, the voice that begins with "I feel" was one of my inauthentic voices. In the past, I would catch myself saying it and try to rephrase. Now, I simply accept the statements I make, the actions I take, and my life decisions. I feel truly liberated from the extreme level of thought control and hyper-analysis I previously subjected myself to.

I feel healthier than ever, both physically and psychologically, and I'm hopeful for the future. So much of my identity was wrapped up in Human Design. I had the sense that my entire life was somehow on a track. I no longer feel that way. I don't know what the future holds—and I'm okay with that.

Ironically, in describing my experience to others in Human Design, most immediately reframe it as an example of me living my design even more fully. They say things like, "The fact that you don't know is healthy," or "Jonah, it sounds like you were stuck in the mind, and now you've finally surrendered to the form." Or, "You were trying to achieve something with your Undefined Ego, and now you've let go."

I'm not going to police how other people see the world. But to me, those descriptions are banal—and frankly, insulting to the intelligence of anyone who actually takes language and thought seriously. I won't police how anyone else thinks, but I no longer see the world that way.

I don't believe my current state is the result of overcoming the not-self, or surrendering to the form, or any of that. To me, those slogans are all part of the same cultic thought control that I'm grateful to have escaped. For others who use that language, maybe they aren't as enslaved by those thought-terminating clichés as I was—or maybe they just don't realize it. It's not really my business to speculate.

But if you are someone who explains everything through the Human Design System—including even my departure from it—I would simply ask you to consider whether you might, without realizing it, be under a subtle form of brainwashing. Ask yourself if you have succumbed to a level of thought control that reframes everything through the identitarian logic of an authoritarian system. Even if you don't experience it as authoritarian, you may unknowingly perpetuate it for others.

Then again, it's not my place to say. I am simply relieved to have left Human Design.

Glossary

4% of 4%

Around 12 million people worldwide, or 1-in-625 people, who are at the mutative, elite vanguard of humanity.

Activation

The equivalent of definition but for gates. A gate can be activated or unactivated. Gate activations occur because of the positions of planets at the time of birth and a secondary time (the "design date"), when the Sun was 88° before its position at birth.

Ajna

The center that has a theme of knowing, answering, thinking, logic, and abstraction, with a not-self theme of thinking about things that don't matter.

Analyst

The term of choice for Human Design readers. Analysts can be certified by organizations such as IHDS.

Aura

The aura is said to be an invisible part of the human body that stretches one arm's length beyond your outstretched arm in all directions.

Aura Type

Usually just called type, the aura type is whether someone is a Generator, Projector, Manifestor, or Reflector. (Sometimes the

Manifesting Generator is considered a fifth type, though this is debated.)

Authority

A person's "authority," or inner authority, is said to be the one surefire thing they can trust to always make the right decision, every time. Unfortunately, there is much debate about how to know when you are trusting your authority versus trusting conditioning or the not-self construct.

Base theory

An aspect of Human Design study involving fundamental dimensions of the universe, referred to as the biverse.

Binary

See: Dualism.

Bodygraph

The diagram used in Human Design to show centers, channels, and gates.

Biverse

Ra's name for the universe, indicating its binary nature.

Bridging gate

An unactivated gate that, if activated, would connect two separate areas of definition (four or more centers). Bridging gates can have not-self themes like centers do.

Calm eater

One of twelve configurations of determination. Calm eaters, also called calm touch, are supposed to eat sitting down in calm environments without being bothered by others. Talking to others or even sitting in aura with them may be considered disturbing to the requirement of calm.

Carry

To have a particular line in your profile, e.g. the 1/4, 2/4, 4/1, and 4/6 profiles "carry" the 4th line.

Center

An energy center in the body similar to a chakra from the Vedic chakra system. We are said to have nine centers: Head, Ajna, Throat, Ego, G Center, Solar Plexus, Spleen, Sacral, and Root. Centers can have not-self themes.

Channel

Two gates that are "harmonic" to each other, linking two centers together.

Chart

See: Bodygraph.

Choicelessness

A concept in Human Design that we live in a choiceless existence. See: No choice.

Clean

When the centers operate cleanly, they put out a frequency that is not distorted.

Cognition

The "cognitive architecture" or sensory superpower that most people are not tapping into. Supposedly, by living your design, you unlock this superpower.

Collective (circuitry)

One of three circuit groups. Collective circuitry is about impersonal sharing with strangers and the universal subject, and is divided between logic (understanding) and abstract (experiential) circuits.

Color

One of six subdivisions within each line. Colors are interpreted variously as indicating a person's determination (or PHS), environment, view or perspective, and motivation.

Conditioning

Outside influences that we absorb and internalize, pulling us away from making decisions according to our inner authority.

Correct

A special term used to denote what is in accordance with inner authority and the true self.

Cross of Planning

An incarnation cross having to do with community, working together, institutions, skill, and details.

Cross of the Sleeping Phoenix

An incarnation cross known for being individualistic (see Individual circuitry), among other themes. Our global cycle is said to shift into the theme of the Cross of the Sleeping Phoenix on February 15, 2027.

Crystals of consciousness

In rave cosmology, the crystals of consciousness were originally two main crystals that shattered in the Big Bang. Each one of us is claimed to have a personality crystal and a design crystal that act as filters of neutrinos and orchestrators of consciousness on earth. Ra said we should not think of them as literal crystals but rather having a crystalline structure, and intimated they may be made of dark matter, making them impossible to detect by normal means. He claimed they were a few neutrino widths wide.

Crystal, design

The design crystal is claimed to be the seat of our unconscious mind and in charge of the wellbeing of the body. Each design crystal only incarnates once before returning to the design crystal bundle in the earth's mantle.

Crystal, personality

The personality crystal is the seat of the conscious mind and what we would generally consider the characteristics of our personality. It is something akin to the eternal soul which reincarnates lifetime after lifetime.

Deconditioning
A process of slowly shedding not-self themes and mental interference, facilitated by following strategy and authority. Deconditioning is supposedly a lifelong process, where you can never become fully deconditioned, but you experience a major milestone after the first seven years, and on subsequent cycles every seven years after that.

Defined center
A center in the bodygraph that is colored in, seen as a consistent aspect of a person that is usually relatively impervious to the not-self themes of that center. A defined center is formed when two gates create a channel between that center and another center.

Definition
Refers to the areas of defined centers in the bodygraph.

Definition, single
When all defined centers in a bodygraph are connected by channels.

Definition, split
When there are defined centers in the bodygraph that are not connected contiguously by channels.

Design, the
The concept of the design usually refers to the so-called design side of the bodygraph, colored in red, signifying the unconscious. It can also be used more loosely to refer to a person's body, unconscious, or aspects of the bodygraph.

Designed
This term is usually used to mean what is indicated in the bodygraph. For instance, someone can be *designed for shores,* or *designed to eat single ingredients.*

Design crystal bundle
The design crystal bundle is said to reside in the earth's mantle and act as a planetary intelligence akin to Jung's notion of the collective unconscious.

Design date
The time approximately 3 months before birth when the Sun was 88° before its position at the moment of birth.

Design-side
The design-side of the bodygraph is colored in red and signifies the unconscious.

Determination
Also known as primary health system, or PHS. Refers to a dietary regimen such as eating only one ingredient at a time, eating the same thing over and over, eating only hot or cold foods, and other prescriptions.

Distortion
A term that refers to a particular frequency that is associated with the not-self. Open centers are said to amplify to the point of distortion when operating uncleanly.

Dualism
Ra's worldview is fundamentally binaristic, putting many aspects of reality into opposition, e.g. yin and yang qualities, initiating versus waiting to respond, and dozens of other binaries.

Ego
The center involved with willpower. The not-self theme of the Undefined Ego is trying to prove oneself.

Emotional clarity
Waiting for emotional clarity is the prescribed strategy for those with a Defined Solar Plexus. This means to wait some amount of time until a felt sense of emotional clarity emerges before making decisions.

Environment
The ideal environment that a person is said to meet the least resistance in.

Eron
An immortal form that humans are said to evolve into hundreds of thousands of years in the future.

Experiment, entering into the
Entering into the Human Design experiment, or simply the experiment, means to begin following strategy and authority. It is a marker of the time when deconditioning supposedly begins.

Frequency
A "vibe" that people put off, or an impression they make.

Fractal line
A lineage of connections between people, with the idea of some people being further up or down the fractal line, closer to the source.

G Center
The center associated with identity, love, and direction.

Gate
One of 64 positions in the bodygraph that correspond to the 64 hexagrams of the I'Ching.

Geometry
Often referred to as one's unique geometry, this term is essentially interchangeable with trajectory as a concept referring to one's path in life.

Generator
One of four aura types in Human Design. The Generator is said to have an encompassing aura generated by their Defined Sacral Center. Their strategy is to wait to respond.

Global cycle
A major theme that lasts approximately 410 years. The current

global cycle, the Cross of Planning, changes to the Cross of the Sleeping Phoenix on February 15, 2027.

Head
The center involved with mental pressure.

IHDS (International Human Design School)
Originally International Human Design Schools (plural), IHDS is an organization devoted to teaching Human Design. They have around 2,100 analysts listed on its website, making it the largest Human Design teaching organization in the world. It was officially sanctioned by Ra Uru Hu following a financial arrangement with its founder, Lynda Bunnell.

Incarnation cross
An aspect of the bodygraph that supposedly yields archetypal themes related to life purpose.

Individual (circuitry)
One of the three circuit groups along with collective and tribal, related specifically to mutation and melancholy, with a keynote of empowerment.

In aura
Within the aura space of another; within the space around one arm's length past their outstretched arm.

Initiating
Taking action to start something. For all aura types other than the Manifestor, initiating is seen as an expression of the not-self.

Inner Authority
See: Authority.

Jovian Archive
An organization formed by Ra Uru Hu to further his teachings. Unlike IHDS, Jovian does not certify Human Design analysts.

Keynote
A keyword given by Ra for a particular aspect of the Human Design System.

Killer monkey
Ra uses this term to refer to the seven-centered form.

Leftness
A way of processing information strategically that has been around for thousands of years. An evolutionary leftover from the seven-centered era.

Line
There are six lines within each gate, corresponding to the lines of the hexagrams of the I'Ching.

Living your design
A catch-all term for following your strategy and authority.

Maya, the
Ra's term to refer to the entirety of existence, or the universe. Often stylized *maia*.

Mechanics
A reference to how things ostensibly function in the world, often described as the mechanics of aura type, or the mechanics of the maya.

Meeting Human Design
To "meet" HD, also known as entering into the experiment, is the moment a person begins to follow their strategy and authority.

Mental interference
Decision-making is seen as a battle between mental interference (the mind making decisions) versus a more authentic way of arriving at decisions using inner authority. Mental interference is how the not-self influences decision-making.

Mental stories
It is a commonplace in Human Design to tell someone the mind is making up stories when they raise questions or concerns.

Mindy
Mentally-driven, exhibiting mental interference.

Motivation
An aspect of the bodygraph that supposedly shows how a person is motivated, whether by fear, hope, desire, need, guilt, or innocence (the lack of motivation).

Motor
One of the "motorized" centers: Sacral, Root, Solar Plexus, or Ego.

Mutation, mutative
A term denoting either individual circuitry in its propensity for creativity, or the 4% of the 4%, elite vanguard of humanity bringing about new cultural forms. Sometimes also used to indicate the supposed work of evolution in bringing about new forms like the rave.

Nine-centered, nine-centered form
A new evolution in the human organism with nine energy centers instead of seven, emerging in 1781. In practice, nine-centered is used to mean something like honoring and respecting each other's individual empowerment and ability to trust their own inner authority.

No choice
An oft-repeated slogan that is sometimes used to indicate a belief in fatalism or predeterminism.

Non-sacral types
Projectors, Manifestors, and Reflectors.

Not my fractal
A dismissive statement used to indicate dislike or inability to connect with a person.

Not-self
A catch-all term for a secondary consciousness within a person that is the result of conditioning and openness.

Not-self theme (aura type)
A frequency of frustration, bitterness, anger, or disappointment, depending on aura type.

Not-self theme (center)
A particular fixed pattern that undefined centers and bridging gates have.

Not-self theme (bridging gate)
The not-self theme of a bridging gate is a pull of conditioning on people who are split definition into the not-self.

Open center
An undefined center. (Sometimes used to mean an undefined center with no activations.)

Operating
Jargon to refer to whether a person is operating from their true self (with an accompanying frequency of satisfaction, success, peace, or surprise) or if they are operating from the not-self.

Personality, the
The concept of the personality in Human Design can either refer to the personality crystal, one of two crystals of consciousness each person is said to have, or the personality-side activations in the bodygraph.

Personality-side
The personality-side of the bodygraph is colored in black and signifies the conscious mind.

Perspective
See: View.

Profile
An aspect of the bodygraph that describes a person's supposed role in the totality.

Projection field
Also called the 5th line projection field, an idea that people who "carry" 5th lines in their profile (i.e. the 2/5, 3/5, 5/1, and 5/2 profiles) attract psychological projections from others.

Projector
An aura type with a focused aura that can X-ray the other person. Told to wait for invitations.

Projector ascendancy
The idea that Projectors are meant to be our guides into the future and are ascending to their rightful place at the top of the hierarchy as leaders of culture.

Quad right
Someone who has four right variable placements in their bodygraph.

Rave
Originally a word Ra used to describe the nine-centered form. Later, Ra began describing a new form that would emerge in the future, post-2027, bearing psychic abilities and other unusual characteristics.

Rave cosmology
The study of cosmology through the lens of Human Design.

Rave mandala
An arrangement of hexagrams in a wheel according to the Shao Yong (also called Fu Xi) binary sequence.

Reflector
An aura type with a sampling, "teflon" aura. Told to wait a full lunar cycle before making a decision.

Resistance, meeting

Meeting resistance is a catch-all term for coming up against struggles in life that are said to diminish health, longevity, and lead to the not-self theme of the aura type: frustration, bitterness, anger, or disappointment.

Rightness

A new form of intelligence that is receptive rather than strategic. A word Ra used to describe the way in which a "right" person (those with right-facing variable arrows) perceives and processes information: more passive, receptive, and broad in focus, compared to "leftness."

Right variable

One of the four possible facing directions of the variable arrows in the bodygraph. A right variable is said to be more receptive, less strategic, and more open-ended than a left variable in that same position.

Root

The center of adrenaline and pressure.

Sacral

Described as the life force energy of the planet, the Sacral Center is associated with fertility and exerting energy.

Sacral response

A yes/no response to a stimulus experienced by those with a Defined Sacral Center, often accompanied by sacral sounds.

Sacral sounds

Vocalized sounds like "uh huh" and "uh uh" that supposedly indicate correct and incorrect decisionmaking for Generators.

Sacral types

Generators and Manifesting Generators. (Note: Ra purists will either include Manifesting Generators as a type of Generator rather than a distinct type, or no distinction will be made at all.)

Shores
One of six primary environments that people can be designed to live in.
Solar Plexus
The emotional center.
Source
Sometimes referring to source knowledge, or an abstract idea of the source of all intelligence and information in the universe, i.e. God.
Source knowledge
Knowledge that directly comes from Ra and, ostensibly, his encounter with the Voice.
Spleen
The center associated with security and, when not-self, holding onto things that aren't good for you.
Surrender
A major concept in Human Design; it means to give up mental control and surrender to inner authority.
Throat
The center of communication, action, metamorphosis, and initiating.
Trajectory
One's life path.
Variable
Arrows in the bodygraph signifying where you have leftness or rightness.
Voices of the Throat
Ways of talking, some of which will be "true self" and some not-self depending on activations in the chart.

Acknowledgements

I would like to thank my parents Dreama and John, min älskling love of my life Lina, my step-mom Annette, brother and sister Max & Emma, Dempcy family Birney, Marie, Di, Peter and Bob, Blankenbeckler family Kurt, Linda, Tomas, Amanda, Keith, Debbie, Adam and Abby, and my friends and loved ones—Jonny & Aron, Mike & Diana, David & Karina, Von Paul, Hilda & Jeff, Ray-O-Light, David W., Kirby, Ka Li Ma & Joe, Danny, Alex Grande, Cary, Angie, Taylor Ames, Oscar, Richard & Brandy, Genoa & Lasita, Matthew & Abigail, Lolo & Derek, Krista, George, Ramon, Raphael, Singh, Shango, Kira, Michel, Blossom, Erin, Kaisie, C Alex Clark, Fujio & Monica, Liliana, Joe, Hanifa, Ashley Gray Duncan, Lyra Salandre, Rebekah Francis Cantor, Sabina, Eve, Téo, Jon, Holly, Sophia, Meena, Brooke, Veronica, Dani, Victoria, Mark Germain, Roger, Swiss Mike, Sean W., Sean M., Maddie, Orion, Lynda, Jess Tilly, Jess Levy, Sarah Kim, John and Amy, Bri, Travis, Russell, Seven, Debe, Indra, Milana, Lindsey & Julia, Courtney & Garrett, Brett & Taylor, Meher, Marissa, Susie & Karl, Augustina, Iris, Feliciano, Monique & Amy, Bryan, Alex Negrete, Minkyu, Kimberly, Stephanie A., Stephanie C., Nicola, Micah, Patrick, Olivia, Jaco, Caslon & Lindsay, Karen & Colin, Taea, Dave, Dietrie, Doc, Teresa, Brandy G., James & Kara, Collyn, Moniste, Adrienne, Mary, Jannica & Abe, Larry, Peter, Andre, Chiara G., B., and L., Shay, Eve, and my Ibiza friends Billy, Sonja, and Bamboo.

231

www.ingramcontent.com/pod-product-compliance
Lightning Source LLC
Chambersburg PA
CBHW022015090426
42739CB00006BA/139